TRAVELLERS IN SPAIN

Spain seen through the eyes of famous travellers,
from Borrow to Hemingway

◆

DAVID MITCHELL

SANTANA BOOKS

First published in 1988.
This edition published in 2004
by Santana Books.

Designed by Andrea Carter.
Cover photograph by David Baird.
Photographs: Bengt Adin 122, Gerald Brenan Archives 127,
AGE Fotostock 128, Laurie Lee Estate 155, J.D. Dallet 182.

Travellers in Spain
is published by Ediciones Santana S.L.,
Apartado 422, Fuengirola 29640 (Málaga) Spain.
Tel. 952 485 838. Fax 952 485 367.
info@santanabooks.com
www.santanabooks.com

Printed in Spain by Gráficas San Pancracio S.L.,
Poligono Industrial San Luis, Málaga.

Depósito Legal: MA-590/2004
ISBN 84-89954-33-X

CONTENTS

THE QUOTABLE SPAIN

By Tom Burns

Spain has exerted an extraordinary pull on international travellers. Political agents, protestant bible-sellers, dilettantes and society matrons, professional sensation-seekers and soldiers on leave, hopeful *hommes de lettres* and established lions of literary salons, the travellers themselves constitute a motley crew that is worthy of a Chaucerian epic. Britons and Americans, Italians and French, Germans and Scandinavians, they roamed the length and breadth of the peninsula.

Almost as soon as they had reached their first *posada*, they felt compelled to write about their experiences.

The literature that they produced down the ages is vast and it is a treasure trove both for the armchair traveller and for the student of social history. In addition to the adventures, episodes and insights that mark all travel writing, the huge output of the "I went-to-Spain" brigade, when it is taken as a whole, forms a fascinating patchwork of attitudes towards the country they were scrutinizing. The travel literature on Spain tells as much about the evolution of the nation and the society under examination as it does about the changing prejudices, the social manners and the priorities of those who contributed to this exceptional opus of travel writing.

Early travellers moaned about Spain's barbaric backwardness, her discomforts and her dangers. Later writers extolled as romantic virtues the very remoteness and the hazards that their predecessors had wimped about. Increasingly, in an age of reliable trains, central heating and modern policing, recent and contemporary travel writing on Spain mourns the passing of an idealized, sacred and rustic society. Preconceived notions of a nation and of a people supposedly unsullied by modernity have been rudely shattered by the jet engines of mass tourism charter flights.

Why was there this massive movement, by the talented and the talentless alike, to go to Spain and then to explain it to a "civilized" world? David Mitchell, in his exhaustive investigation of those who came and wrote, goes a long way towards providing the answer. He has read just about everything that anyone has ever written about Spain after a sojourn within her borders and he lets each of his grand array of authors speak for himself or herself.

By massing all the travellers together and treating each in turn, Mitchell establishes, tentatively but plausibly, a common ground. What strikes each author about Spain is, in the final analysis, remarkably similar. This ought to be odd since the travellers, mostly individualists, were as chalk and cheese to each other and each reflected the standpoints of a given age and background.

The thread that runs through all the travel writing on Spain consists of a series of variations on the theme of Iberia's real or imagined "difference." This was especially true in the 19th century. It was the exoticism of Spain that, lamp-like, attracted romantics like a horde of so many moths. At a time when the Grand Tour was all the rage, Spain was a cut-price Constantinople, a Byzantine world that was affordable for the adventurer of more moderate means.

Penetrating the Pyrenees, the travellers immediately sensed that they had left Europe behind them. As they pressed south, they entered the barrenness of a sunbaked, limitless table-land whose horizons were punctuated, here and there, by suitably decaying castles and cathedrals; venturing past the brigand-infested sierras, they finally reached the lush lands, the verdant vegas, of Andalusia where men were jealous and where dark-eyed women smouldered to the scent of jasmine and to the tinkling freshness of fountains.

Bowling over the Pyrenees for a Spanish holiday. In the 1870s one disgruntled observer recorded that "old residents and seasoned tourists are beginning to complain of the invasion of the northern hordes."

It really was a world away from the gentle shires. It was "abroad" with a vengeance. It was far removed from a summer spent splashing in Baden Baden, or trekking in the Tyrol or viewing frescos in Florence. A visit to Seville's tobacco factory, where hundreds of Carmens were rolling the leaf, was *de rigueur*. So was an afternoon at the bullfight. A stagecoach rendezvous with a *bandolero* really was something to write home about.

In Mitchell's survey of what the travellers actually produced, it is fairly simple to trace the stages in which the Iberian stereotypes were created. The Spanish canvas became a picaresque pastiche of pride, courage and indolence, sensuality and religious bigotry. The starving grandee clothed only in his dignity, the prostitute who burnt candles to madonnas in her boudoir, delighted those who were determined to establish the "difference" of Spain. Gentlemen could dine out for months before avid audiences on their return from Spain. Authors knew that in Spain they had a subject that would win them new readers.

So utterly exotic was Spain deemed to be by this galaxy of authors that there was a consensus that it would not change. The travellers who had created their image of Spain confidently predicted that no railroads could be built in the rough terrain they had trod and that modern mores would never make inroads on a people that was so essentially at odds with the urbanity of northern climes.

As Mitchell brings the traveller story up to the present day, it is curious to note the ill-disguised churlishness among those who have been forced to recognize that Spain has ceased to be a byzantine bolt-hole for sensation-seekers. Modern day Carmens smoke American filter-tips instead of chewing tobacco and they wear mini-skirts and listen to pop music. The sons, and also the daughters, of the haughty *hidalgos* have MBAs from American universities.

Spain is no longer "different," to the seeming distress of those who were determined that it should be. The society in which time had apparently stood still has become much like that of everywhere else. Worst of all, Spain is no longer a shared secret among *aficionados* and their reading public. In any given year more foreigners visit Spain than there are Spaniards. No longer the subject of a specialist book, Spain has become the picture of a holiday postcard.

–Tom Burns

I

FIRST DRAFTS

17th-century travellers

At its peak, after the takeover in 1580 of Portugal and her dominions, the Spanish empire included the whole of South and Central America, a slice of North America, nearly half of Italy, part of the Netherlands, the Philippines, Ceylon, the Congo and various settlements from the East Indies to the Azores and the Caribbean.

But superpower prominence meant interminable wars, grinding taxation, and an ever-present threat of internal revolt. The papacy joined a long list of enemies when Philip II, the monk-king of the Escorial, made it clear that he regarded the extirpation of the Lutheran heresy as a specifically Spanish, or Habsburg, concern. Spain's heroic Golden Age was a period of increasingly desperate one-against-all improvisations.

The humiliating failure of the Armada in 1588 was the first ominous crack in the legend of Spanish invincibility.

An anonymous Italian priest who travelled with a papal delegation in the 1590s took obvious pleasure in mocking the vulnerable, though still formidable and feared, colossus. Rome, he reflected, was after all the religious and cultural capital of Europe, Italy the prime destination for all serious tourists—including Spaniards. The fact was that despite a monopoly of New World treasure only Italian bankers' loans kept the Spanish crown precariously solvent and Spanish armies in the field.

The destruction of the Armada in 1588 was the first omen of Spain's vulnerability as a superpower. "God blew and they were scattered" said an exultant English slogan.

His experiences on the mission confirmed his sense of superior sophistication. The mid-winter journey from Barcelona to Madrid took three weeks. The roads were frightful, the inns fireless, and there was only straw (usually verminous) to sleep on. When lice and bugs had done their worst there was the danger of being robbed by brigands from filthy, kennel-like villages (a state of affairs which, according to contemporary reports, was much the same in many parts of Italy). And what of Madrid? Decreed into existence as his administrative capital by Philip II because of its remoteness and symbolically central site, it was still little more than a raw, new town with few pretensions to elegance.

The priest thought it unbelievably squalid and uncouth. Houses of dried mud, often of only one storey. No chimneys or privies.

"On this account they do their business in pots, which they empty out of their windows. This creates an intolerable stench... If they were not diligent to clean the streets it would be impossible to pass through them, but withal it is impossible to go on foot."

Except for the lucky few who had been civilized by residence in Italy, Spaniards seemed to lack any sense of delicacy. In Madrid men and women urinated in the street without regard to passers-by. Their table manners were disgusting. Ignorant of the use of knives and forks, they dipped their fingers in a common dish. How absurd it was, how unfair, that such barbarians should be so powerful.

Sir Charles Cornwallis, sent as English ambassador after the peace treaty of 1604 had ended decades of warfare, was no more complimentary. He groaned as he bumped over rutted tracks en route from La Coruña, and a few months later reported that "this estate is one of the most confined and disordered in Christendom." Madrid had only just been reinstated as capital of a thoroughly disunited Spain which, it seemed to Cornwallis, was little more than a fragile federation of semi-autonomous provinces. Philip III, an irresolute weakling, had shifted the choice to Valladolid, only to be lured back to base by a hefty bribe. The treasure of the Indies had been squandered in a vain attempt to uphold imperial prestige. The Cortes of Aragon, Valencia and Catalonia were reluctant to raise money for what they saw as Castile's foreign escapades.

Few except diplomats and merchants braved a distinctly hostile atmosphere. Denunciations of English heretics were answered by propaganda pamphlets claiming that "this semi-Morisco nation is sprung from the filth and slime of Africa, the base Ottomans and the rejected Jews." All travellers were kept under surveillance by English consuls, who reported their movements and contacts. They were also shadowed by agents of the Inquisition, some of them exiled English Catholic priests who offered bribes to gain converts. Cornwallis found himself a virtual prisoner in the embassy, a beleaguered Protestant citadel outside which a noisy rabble led by papist expatriates would often collect crying "Heretics! Lutheran dogs! " He could not wait to get back to England.

The advice of Sir Walter Aston, ambassador in the 1620s, to shun religious controversy was boldly ignored by William Lithgow, a combative Scot who achieved a certain fame as "the Martyr of

Málaga." One of the very few freelance "peregrinators" to cross Spain, he had already explored Italy, Greece, Turkey and North Africa before setting out on his third great voyage, planned to take him via Ireland, Spain and Egypt to the legendary land of Prester John, Ethiopia.

Even allowing for the rant of a hyperbolic style, it is evident that Lithgow was no puller of prejudiced, and especially of anti-papist, punches. According to him "the barbarian Moore, the Moorish Spaniard, the Turke and the Irishman are the least industrious and most sluggish livers under the Sunne." Reaching Spain in June 1620, he describes it as "generally a masse of mountains, a barren ill-manured soyle... so desartuous that I have gone two dayes journey unseeing house or village except two ventas (tavernes)... Villages be so farre distant, the rockie Sierras and Alpes so innumerable."

He also gives what is perhaps the first description of a do-it-yourself posada (inn): "No ready drest diet... You must buy first in one place your fire, your meate from the butcher, your wine from the taverne, your fruits, oyle and herbes from the botega, carrying all to your bed-lodging. Thus must the weary stranger toile or else fast. And in infinite places for Gold nor money can have no victuals."

The outlandish rarity of tourists went far to explain such apparent inhospitality. He writes that "the most penurious peasants in the world be heere, whose quotidian moanes might draw teares from stones." Yet he must have been aware of the primitive existence of Scottish Highland peasants, of whom a contemporary chronicler said that "the poorer sort live in such miserable huts as never eye beheld... pigging together in a mousehole of mud, heath and such like matter." And much the same was true of Ireland. But when he wrote up his Spanish recollections Lithgow was not in the mood for careful comparison or balanced judgement.

Arriving in Málaga at the end of October, he was soon in deep trouble. Strolling with sailors ashore from "the English fleete that went against the Pyrats of Algiers," he was suspected of being a spy sent ahead to report the arrival date of the treasure convoy then nearing the Mediterranean (it was believed that the real purpose of the English

Philip III, whose moving of the capital from Madrid to Valladolid and, in 1606, back again (for a hefty bribe), typified the political and economic chaos of Spain's so-called Golden Age.

ships was to plunder this). On the way back to his lodging Lithgow was arrested by "nine Alguazilos... wrapping me up in a blacke frizado cloake and gripping my throate to stop my crying."

He may have exaggerated his "tragicall sufferings" and "Pinnacles of Paine," but the tortures he endured in the next five months left him semi-crippled for life. Examined by experts of the Inquisition—for if he was not a spy he was certainly a contumacious heretic—he was stretched on the rack and horribly distended by the water-ordeal until "mine eyes began to startle, and my mouth to foame, and my teeth to chatter like to the doubling of Drummers stickes." One passage in his confiscated notebooks must have been particularly offensive to his interrogators: "I confess," he had written, "for the Spanish Nunne that she is more holy than the Italian; the former are onely reserved to the friars and priests. The latter, being more Noble, have most affinity with Gentlemen."

Nor did his sarcasms about the Virgin Mary and the Roman Church improve his case. Refusing the offer of money to convert, he was kept in chains and threatened that he "should be transported privately to Granada, and there about midnight to be burnt body and bones into ashes."

Not until Easter 1621 was he released. News of his plight had reached some English merchants in Málaga. They contacted Sir William Aston who, doubtless cursing this troublesome traveller, "mediated with the King and Counsell of Spaine." Back in London he was carried on a stretcher through crowded streets to a royal audience. King James, a fellow Scot who had sponsored his journey, paid for a cure at Bath which helped Lithgow to recover his strength—sufficiently, it seems, to assault the Spanish ambassador, Count Gondomar, when a promise to pay damages of £1,000 was not kept. For this he was imprisoned, and despite several parliamentary petitions never got a penny's compensation.

William Lithgow's account of these events acted as a stiff deterrent to Spanish travel. But James Howell's Spanish commentaries, contained in his *Instructions for Forreine Travel and Familiar Letters*, are very different in tone. Almost as widely travelled as Lithgow, and a better linguist, this sprightly Welshman was also, as a crony of Ben Jonson and other leading writers, master of an easy anecdotal style which made him one of the most popular of 17th century authors.

The Letters were written to friends and patrons during his two Spanish "missions." In 1617 he was sent to arrange for shipment of "the alkali known as baryllia" from Alicante to a glass manufacturer in London. Five years later he was in Madrid to negotiate for the release of a captured English merchant vessel. He mentions bad roads and "uncouth adventures" but does not dwell on this theme, having experienced shoddy inns, appalling roads, and highwaymen in other countries, not least in England, where roads were virtually impassable in winter, inn servants often in league with robbers, and foreign VIPs were provided with anti-bandit escorts.

As with so many northern visitors, it was the balmy south that really took his fancy. Valencia, he wrote, was "one of the noblest cities in all Spaine, situate in a large Vega or Valley... Here are the strongest silks, the sweetest wines, the excellentest almonds, the best oils and

A Corrida in Cadiz, from illustrations in Richard Twiss's travel journal. He was shaken, he said, by the bloodthirsty behaviour of the fair sex at the bullfight.

beautifullest Females, for the prime courtesans in Madrid and else-where are had hence... They commonly call it the second Italy, which made the Moors, whereof many were banished hence to Barbary, to think that Paradise was in that part of the Heavens which hung over this City."

He is less charmed with Madrid, where his negotiations did not go well and the king's new favourite, the Count of Olivares, who granted Howell an interview, "behaved churlishly... he said that when Spaniards had justice in England, we should have justice here." Unlike the Italian priest, however, he does not shudder at the state of the streets, since he considered Paris to be "the filthiest city in Christendom."

He briefly describes a bullfight staged in honour of Prince Charles and the Duke of Buckingham: "A great show of baiting Bulls with Men... Commonly there are men killed at it, therefore there are

Priests appointed to be there ready to confess them. It hath happened that a Bull hath taken up two men upon his horns with their guts dangling about them. The horsemen run with lances and swords, the foot with goads. As I am told, the Pope hath sent divers Bulls against this sport of Bulling, yet it will not be left, the Nation hath taken such an habitual delight in it."

He finds the superstition of Spaniards a more interesting topic. "Some, if they spy two straws or sticks lie crosswise in the street they will take them up and kiss them and lay them down again." Excessive piety had its advantages, "for in their Kalendar above five months of the twelve are devoted to some Saint or other and kept festival; a religion that the London apprentices would like well." But with relish Howell tells the story of a Dominican friar who "in a solemn procession in Alcala had his Stones (testicles) dangling under his habit cut off instead of his pocket by a cut-purse."

He reports that during the reconquest "divers parts North-west kept still under Christian kings, specially Biscay, which was never conquered, as Wales in Britain... and the Biscayners have much analogy with the Welsh... They retain to this day the original language of Spain and are reputed the ancientest Gentry; so that when any is to take the Order of Knighthood there are no Inquisitors appointed to find whether he be clear of the blood of the Moors, as in other places. The King, when he comes upon the confines, pulls off one shoe before he can tread upon any Biscay ground."

To Howell the expulsion of the Moors and of the nominally Christian Moriscos had been a sad mistake: "Tis true that the colonizing of the Indies and the wars of Flanders have much drain'd this Country of People; since the expulsion of the Moors it is also grown thinner and not so full of Corn; for those Moors would grub up Wheat out of the very tops of the craggy Hills... so that the Spaniard had nought else to do but to go with his Ass to the Market and buy Corn of the Moors."

A brilliant and, by contrast with Lithgow, unbilious generalizer, Howell's summary of the Spanish temperament heavily

The shrewd writings of James Howell, a Welshman who travelled widely in Spain during the early 17th century, greatly influenced later generalizations about the Spanish temper, from pride-in-poverty to the *mañana* mentality.

influenced subsequent writers. National pride was evident in a much-quoted proverb to the effect that "God created the world in Spanish, Satan beguiled Eve in Italian, and Adam begged pardon in French." Seeping down from the nobility, a contempt for work, the result of a long reliance on Jewish and Moorish "slaves," had, he thought, affected all ranks of society. Poverty was not seen as a disgrace; self-esteem, inflated by a belief that the conquest of the Incas and the Aztecs and the flow of New World bullion were marks of God's favour to his Chosen People, was ever-present and sometimes overweening. "I was told of a Spaniard, who having got a fall by a stumble and broke his nose, rose up and in a disdainful manner said, *Voto a tal esto es caminar por la tierra*, This it is to walk upon earth."

Being of what Howell calls "a goatish race" it was to be expected that a Spaniard would be "a great servant of ladies," though "not so smooth and oily as the Italian." As for the females, "there is a saying that makes a compleat woman, let her be English to the neck, French to the waste, and Dutch below; I may add, for hands and feet let her be Spanish, for they have the least of any. They have another saying, a Frenchwoman in a dance, a Dutchwoman in the kitchen, an Italian in a window, an England-woman at board, and the Spanish a-bed." But one had to bear in mind that "after thirty they are commonly past child-bearing, and I have seen women in England look as youthful at fifty as some here at twenty-five."

Offering practical advice to travellers, Howell warns them to be prepared for delays ("he that hath to deale with that Nation must have good store of Phlegme and patience... for anyone to prescribe a precise time to conclude any businesse there is to reckon without one's host"). But he rates Spain as "the fittest country to see next after France." Don't, he says, be put off by French sarcasm caused by envy of Spain's imperial stature. Take heart that Spanish is "the easiest of all Languages... nought else but mere Latin, take a few Morisco words away," easily distinguished by their guttural pronunciation. True, there was "the Bascuence or Cantabrian tongue" in the north; the speech of Valencia and Catalonia was mingled with French and Italian; and "in the Mountaines of Granada, that last part of Spaine that was inhabited by the Moors, they speak Morisco." But for all practical purposes, the Castilian, or "Christian," tongue would serve.

The traveller should "take heed of Posting in that hot country in the Summer time, for it may stirre the masse of blood too much," and should expect tough going and wide climatic swings: "for about the third part of the peninsula is made up of huge craggy Hills and Mountaines, amongst which one shall feele in some places more difference in point of temper of heat and cold in the ayre than twixt Winter and Summer under other Climes." The autumn was the time "to make the journey to South Spain to see Seville and the Contratation House of the West Indies."

Though much of the silver from the fleets which anchored each year in the port of Sanlucar de Barrameda went to foreign bankers and merchants, enough remained to add a glamour of opulence and gaiety to Seville. If, wrote Howell, one could contrive to be there in October "at the arrival of the Plate Fleet," he would witness an event which, for excitement and pageantry, was unrivalled in Europe: "such a *Grandeza* that the Roman Monarchy in her highest flourish never had the like, nor the Gran Signor at this day."

For Lady Fanshawe, Seville, "that great city, though now much decayed," was remembered in her old age as the place where "the Conde de Molina presented me with a young lion; but I desired his Excellency's pardon that I did not accept of it, saying I was of so cowardly a nature I durst not keep company with it." Gifts had been showered upon her and her husband Sir Richard (newly-appointed ambassador) from the moment when they arrived at Cadiz in 1664.

"The English consul with all the merchants brought us a present of two silver basins and ewers, with a hundredweight of chocolate and crimson taffeta clothes." At Jerez the Duchess of Albuquerque received them, "placing me on her right hand upon cushions, as the fashion of this Court is." Lady Fanshawe explains that women seldom ate with their husbands, or if they did they sat cross-legged (Moorish-style) on the floor with their children, being unused to sitting on chairs, which they found uncomfortable. Cushions were used only for ceremonial occasions, the number provided indicating rank, as when at an audience in the Buen Retiro palace Lady Fanshawe saw the queen "seated under a cloth of state on three cushions."

In Madrid she thought the women "most witty in repartees... They all paint white and red from the Queen to the cobbler's wife, old and young, widows excepted." But she pitied "the children of the greatest," who had a miserable upbringing, "kept from conversing with their relatives and friends, never eating with their parents" and left in the charge of a gloomy priest. "Until their daughters marry they never stir so much as downstairs, nor marry for any consideration under their own quality, which to prevent, if their fortunes will not procure, they make them nuns."

A special delight was to travel with Spaniards, for then, perhaps because it was such a rare event, "they are the most jolly persons in the world, dealing their provisions of all sorts to every person they meet when they are eating." Indeed Lady Fanshawe, who had known very hard times during the English civil war and as a royalist exile, is almost breathlessly eloquent about Spanish provisions, firmly refuting "the received opinion that Spain affords not food either

Granada—one of Henry Swinburne's illustrations of the Alhambra in
his "Travels Through Spain" (1777). Great-great-grandfather to the
poet Algernon Swinburne, his book is full of spicy detail,
not least about idle, dissolute monks.

good or plentiful." If one had "skill to choose and money to buy...
there is not in the Christian world better wines than their midland
wines, besides sherry and Canary. Their water tastes like milk and their
wheat makes the sweetest and best bread in the world; bacon beyond
belief good, Segovia veal much larger and fatter than ours... the best
partridges I ever ate and the best sausages... The cream is much sweeter
and thicker than any I ever saw in England; their eggs much exceed
ours; and so all sorts of sallads and roots and fruits... and olives which
are nowhere so good..."

But Lady Fanshawe's memoir was not intended for publica-
tion. The best-seller of the century was by a Frenchwoman, Mme
d'Aulnoy. A talented writer best known for her fairy stories (notably
Goldilocks), her version of Spanish high society is much spicier. Full of

Gallic condescension as France under Louis XIV became Europe's dominant power, she saw Spain as at best semi-civilized—but rather quaintly, excitingly so. During the next 150 years her book, first published in 1691, was frequently reprinted in several languages and often quoted as totally authentic. Yet she probably never set foot in Spain, using bona fide travelogues, court gazettes, and bulletins from her mother, who had fled to Madrid to avoid criminal prosecution.

Some of her baroque set-pieces might have been lifted from the more extravagant plays of Calderón. At a *fiesta de toros* in Madrid's Plaza Mayor a handsome young *hidalgo* (bullfighting was then a sport for nobles), showing off to impress his ladylove, is horribly gored to death. A jealous woman gives her husband his mistress's heart to eat. Another, dressed in men's clothes, fights and wounds a faithless lover. Hired *bravoes* are told exactly what kind of wounds to inflict. Amorous intrigue is perpetual and usually ends in several fatalities.

Concentrating on the foibles of the idle rich, she describes the antics of dandified penitents in Holy Week: "I thought I should swoon away... Fancy a man coming so near you that he'll cover you all over with blood... There are certain rules by which to discipline themselves elegantly, and masters to teach the art, just as to dance and fence... On the back of their waistcoats they have two great holes, and a ribbon tied to their whip. Commonly 'tis their mistress which honours them with this favour."

Idleness bred dissipation ("even youths of quality begin at the age of 12 or 13 years to entertain a concubine") and syphilis was so common that it was taken for granted. "Their children either bring it into the world from their mother's womb or suck it from the nurse; a virgin may be justly suspected to have it; and they are hardly persuaded to be cured of it, they are so certain of falling again into the same condition... At Court, and amongst the women of the highest quality, they discourse of it as they do of a fever or the megrim."

Since few Spaniards ever went abroad, ignorance of the world had fostered the delusion that Spain, and especially Madrid, was "the very centre of all glory and happiness." Yet the fact was that "fewer strangers come to Madrid than to any capital city"; and this was hardly surprising, for "they'll run the hazard of being very ill-lodged. Spaniards are not ready to offer their houses to anybody because of their wives, of whom they are extreme jealous... and I do not know that there's any more than two inns, whereof at one of them they eat after the French mode... Add to this that there's no convenience for passing to and fro. Hackney coaches are scarce."

Yet Mme d'Aulnoy could not help admiring the sublime fecklessness of grandees who "after pillaging their subjects, spend freely with never a thought of investments, for they think it below 'em to improve their money... One prince who hath places and commissions to dispose of at Seville had rather lose their value than set his hand to the necessary dispatches, saying that it is not agreeable to the generosity of such a caballero to trouble himself to sign his name for so small a matter."

Not long after this narrative appeared, Daniel Defoe, who had not visited the country either, epitomized Spain thus in a rollicking verse satire:

> Pride, the first peer and president of hell,
> To his share Spain, the largest province, fell.
> The subtle prince thought fittest to bestow
> On these the golden mines of Mexico,
> With all the silver mountains of Peru...
> Because he knew their genius to be such,
> Too lazy and too haughty to be rich.
> Too proud a people, so above their fate,
> That if reduced to beg, they'll beg in state.
> Lavish of money to be counted brave,
> And proudly starve because they scorn to save.
> Never was nation in the world before
> So very rich and yet so very poor.

SPAIN REDISCOVERED

18th-century travellers

"No more Pyrenees," Louis XIV is supposed to have said when in 1700 his teenage grandson became king of Spain as Philip V and French appointees began to infiltrate the Royal Council.

But almost immediately, determined that Spain and her empire should not be virtually controlled by France, England and Holland backed the claim of Archduke Charles of Austria to the throne. Lured by a promise that their "rights and liberties from the King of Spain" would be "settled on a lasting foundation," Catalonia (which in the 1640s had fought for independence with French military aid), Aragon and Valencia joined the anti-Bourbon coalition. French, English, Dutch and German armies poured into Spain. When the War of the Spanish Succession ended in 1713 Philip V was still king, but Spain had been stripped of her European possessions, and Gibraltar, captured in 1704 on behalf of the Austrian pretender, flew the British flag.

There followed yet another strenuous attempt to assert the authority of the central government and to cut through the jungle of *fueros* (traditional feudal rights). By the 1760s it seemed just possible that Spaniards (though, as Charles III put it, "they cried when they had their faces washed") might at last be edged into the European mainstream by the wellmeaning decrees of this "enlightened despot," advised by "experts" who, even if Spanish, were guided by the anti-clerical rationalism of Voltaire and the French *philosophes*. The Jesuits were expelled, the power of the Church curbed, education secularized, grandiose economic schemes launched. Curious to see how the reformist regime would fare, foreign travellers came in greater numbers, and thanks to a spate of detailed and sometimes brilliant travelogues, many of them by British writers, Spain crept on to the Grand Tour map.

The Rev Edward Clarke, chaplain to the Embassy, rejoiced that the Inquisition "had left off roasting heretics" and that "the more refined manners of France have passed over the Pyrenees." At court it seemed that "even the Spanish language is making its last struggles against the more insinuating one of France... the *mustacho* has dropped from the lip and the cloke from the shoulders of the *noblesse.*"

Writing of Granada, Clarke magnanimously conceded that "had it but a river like the Guadalquivir nothing could exceed it, unless it were an English prospect of the Thames from Cliffden or the Trent from Clifton"; and he was one of the first commentators to extol the merits of Velazquez and Murillo: "It seems to me to be a great error in imagining Italy to be the only school for great painters: Spain, if visited by some of our artists, would, I am persuaded, open new, astonishing and unexamined treasures to their view."

William Beckford, a whimsical millionaire aesthete who travelled in style with a supply of oriental rugs ("essential in protecting my feet from damp brick floors. I spread them all around and they make a flaming exotic appearance."), wanted Spain to be exotically different. His wild enthusiasm during an impromptu *flamenco* session at the Duchess of Osuna's mansion in Madrid annoyed his hostess, who thought it an uncivilized taste, and drew a playful rebuke from Luigi Boccherini, the Italian court composer: "That an Englishman should encourage these inveterate barbarians in such absurdities! There's a chromatic scream! Why this is worse that a convulsive hiccup!" And Beckford was delighted when the prior of the Jeronomite monastery in the Escorial solemnly displayed its most remarkable treasure, "lying upon a quilted satin mattress... a feather from the wing of the Archangel Gabriel, full three feet long and of a blushing hue..."

Alexander Jardine, a former army officer who in 1787, when Beckford was touring, had long been consul at La Coruña, thought Spaniards "the best sort of people under the worst kind of government" and did not welcome a "French" dictatorship, however enlightened. An ardent advocate of free trade, he was also influenced by the burgeoning Romantic movement with its idealization of Nature.

"The very name of Spain," he writes, "awakens in the mind ideas of something romantic and uncommon." In sharp contrast to French worldliness, Spain offered "more of pure nature, sincerity, and sound sense." Its ruins—"so many old castles, declining towns and mansions, the sad remains of former grandeur"—appealed to the imagination, as did the rugged sierras, equally rugged peasants, and the fact that ways of life elsewhere dead or dying were still in full vigour ("we have the advantage of a kind of living history").

French observers were less tolerant of backward, ungrateful Spain. Father Labat, a Dominican missionary who visited Andalusia in 1705, reported that hostility to foreigners, and especially to the French, was widespread, not least among the friars of the convent in Cadiz which was his base. Not, like Beckford, a connoisseur of eccentricity, he was amazed that they should propagate such absurd legends as that "the ship in which the prophet Jonah fled God's presence was from Cadiz; that the Three Wise Men were Spanish kings who sailed from Cadiz to the Holy Land; and that St James, the alleged apostle of Spain, travelled from Tyre in a Cadizian vessel and disembarked at Cadiz."

Labat also complains of the failure to eradicate Islamic superstitions. "Though women—a Moorish custom—sit crosslegged on cushions like tailors, they take great care to hide their feet. For a woman who allows a man to see her feet indicates that she is willing to grant *les derniéres faveurs*." This irrational veto extended to the clergy, the third sex. He had been reprimanded for hoisting his habit in a muddy street.

An artist's impression of the Venetian adventurer Giacomo Casanova roaming Madrid during his "miserable year" (1767-8) in Spain. Twice jailed, he predicted that the country would be "shaken by a furious revolution."

He was horrified by local cattle-slaughtering methods; a kind of impromptu *corrida* with bulls or cows done to death in public by fierce dogs and butcher-picadors ("no wonder the meat is so tough"), and noted that when it came to facing human enemies Spaniards showed little energy. The ragged, unpaid troops sent to recapture Gibraltar were more likely to turn bandit than to do their military duty. Admittedly Ceuta, a remnant of former conquests in North Africa, was still stoutly defended against Muslim assaults. But that was because without Ceuta there would be no excuse for the "Bull of Crusade" tax so vital to the royal treasury. What could one say of a financial system that relied on such a farcical pretence, using the Church to threaten non-contributors with ex-communication and to reward contributors with purgatory cuts and permission to eat butter and cheese in Lent?

Labat, who sometimes slept in the open rather than risk the dirt and discourtesy of the inns, thought Andalusians bone idle and, what was worse, proud of it. "Certain of finding bread and soup at the doors of the convents" (a deplorable encouragement of pauperized vice), "they prefer to live in shameful shabbiness rather than labour to avoid it." Only the despised foreigners deigned to work: not only French, Dutch and English merchants but French watercarriers, street vendors, agricultural labourers and keepers of the only tolerable inns. Labat found only two things to praise: the view of the African coast from Tarifa, and *alpargatas*—rope-soled sandals which he had found excellent for rough walking. "Despite such pleasure as came my way," he icily concludes, "I was not sorry to leave Spain."

Jean-Francois Bourgoing, a career diplomat attached to the French embassy in the 1780s, admits that the predominance of foreigners—Italian, Dutch and Irish, as well as French—at court, at the head of government departments, and in military commands was such as to justify resentment. But he too is exasperated by an obstinate refusal to bow to "progress" and accept the norms of civilized behaviour. The sensuality of the *fandango* and the *volero* was an affront to decency, "re-animating the blunted senses of old age." In some theatres, gypsies ("a class of people of whom society should long since have been purified") were loudly applauded "in parts the effect of which is to make vice familiar by decorating it with the flowers of mirth." Even at fashionable *tertulias* the conversational tone would too often descend from acceptable vivacity into noisy buffoonery. Then there was what seemed to him a cringing addiction to "religious mummery... When priests are met in the streets, the people form a line and give them the wall... If a gentleman in his carriage meets a priest carrying the Host, he gets out and offers him a place... The ludicrous appears when the Host passes a theatre. As soon as the little bell is heard the play is instantly stopped. Spectators and actors, whatever their parts, Moors, Jews or even devils, all without exception turn towards the street door and remain kneeling as long as the bell can be heard."

Of course there were some enlightened Spaniards who "sighed to see superstition still so deeply rooted, just as they lamented the popularity of bullfights. But though one often heard ribald tales about the clergy, the monkish habit was so respected that "a preservative virtue is attributed to it, even beyond this life. Nothing is more common than to see the dead buried in a friar's dress"; and Franciscan convents in particular did a brisk trade from "a special warehouse appropriated to this posthumous wardrobe." Bourgoing claims to have seen four-year-old boys dressed as monks playing in the streets. Sometimes their parents would chastise them. And this, he sarcastically comments, "is perhaps the only outrage the habit receives in Spain; and these innocent creatures are the only monks who submit to the austerities of penance."

To the Venetian adventurer Giacomo Casanova, expelled from Vienna and Paris in quick succession, Spain was something of a last resort; and he saw little sign of France's civilizing influence during the "miserable year" (1767-8) he spent there. The Inquisition was still very active, even insisting, he says, that there should be no locks on the inside of bedroom doors in *posadas*. And after seeing female pilgrims on the road wearing Capuchin habits, he reflected that "the idea of pleasing God by wearing monkish garb seems very odd indeed."

Twice jailed—in Madrid and in Barcelona—he did not prosper financially or sexually (then in his forties, he laments that "with me the age of miracles was past"). There were some delights, among them watching and learning to dance the *fandango* ("everything is represented, from the sigh of desire to the final ecstasy; it is a very history of love"); but far more humiliations. And disappointment, too. He was forced to humour the pretensions of a cobbler whose daughter he hoped to seduce and who refused to make him a pair of shoes because "he considered himself an *hidalgo*, and if he were to take anyone's measure he would have to touch his foot, and that would be degrading." Even whores were fussily superstitious, to the point of denouncing as an atheist a client who laughed at the absurdity of covering a picture of Christ or the Virgin before getting down to business.

Casanova's application for the post of governor of a proposed agricultural colony of Swiss immigrants at La Carolina, near Jaen, for which he had been short-listed after impressing the royal ministers by dashing off a libretto for an Italian opera, was unsuccessful; perhaps because he insisted that the Inquisition should be banned from the colony and argued that it would be better to people it with hard-working Asturians or Galicians. Narrowly escaping assassination in Barcelona, and again as he crossed the Pyrenees into France ("where a foreigner is a sacred being"), he had few fond memories.

"Wretched Spain!" he wrote in his memoirs, "your case is too far gone for gentle methods. It needs the cautery and the fire. Your fatal lethargy and foolish pride will be shaken by a furious revolution, a terrible shock, a reconquest of regeneration!"

Madrid, said Casanova, had been "the dirtiest, smelliest town in Europe" until an Italian engineer had designed a sewerage system to make it more or less fit for human habitation. And in 1760, before this improvement, Joseph Baretti, born in Turin but long resident in England, described the city as "a Cloaca Maxima that gives strangers the headache. The abominable ordure scarce leaves a passage to pedestrians alongside the walls... To that the physicians attribute a mortal kind of gripes. Another effect is that it spoils the teeth of the inhabitants. A great pity, especially with regard to the women."

In 1774 sanitation still left much to be desired, according to Major William Dalrymple. "The middling people," he wrote, "live on separate floors, in flats, as in Edinburgh, which renders the one common entrance very dirty... The portals are the receptacles for any kind of filth, since the Spaniard performs the offices of nature behind the gate—a strong remnant of Moorish manners." He also confirms that Mme d'Aulnoy's account of a syphilis-blighted court was no fantasy: "I was presented to a *título* who was almost rotten with the disorder, and his wife, a most agreeable woman, was dying by inches; thus we see half the nobility a diseased and degenerated race."

Of all 18th-century travellers, Joseph Baretti best conveys the sensation of being on the road and among the common people. A distinguished man of letters, he had been encouraged by his friend, the celebrated Dr. Samuel Johnson, to keep a daily travel journal. He

Joseph Baretti, an Italian lexicographer and cultural historian, was encouraged by his friend Dr Samuel Johnson to keep a daily travel journal. Published in 1770, it criticizes the insular prejudice of some English writers on Spain.

made a practice of rising early for long walks, speaking to other wayfarers and rejoining his muleteers for the midday halt. In Extremadura the carriage often capsized: but this, he stoically comments, was to be expected in "a desolate region where few people travel because the roads are bad, and the roads are bad because few people travel."

He found Spanish customs officers less surly and no more corrupt than those in England. And he admired the sobriety of most Spaniards, contrasting it with the sottishness he had seen in England. Irritated by the deliberate procrastination of a corregidor who kept him waiting two days for a permit to travel on to Madrid ("Is Talavera so very bad a town that you should want to leave it in such a hurry?"), he soon recovered his temper listening to the muleteers improvising *seguidillas*. He had thought that "this faculty of singing extempore belonged exclusively to the Italians, or more correctly to the Tuscans," and was surprised that no foreign traveller had yet recorded this national peculiarity.

But perhaps this was not so surprising, since "when they have copied out of each other's books that the Spaniards are proud, grave and idle; the French volatile, confident and talkative; the Italians cunning, jealous and superstitious; and the English rude, inhospitable and phlegmatic; the greatest part of itinerary writers think they have done great matters." Baretti viewed these "propagators of prejudices, falsehoods and calumnies... with the contempt that ought to be the lot of superficial, impertinent and careless observers." And he stoutly denied that Spaniards were inherently idle. They did not work because, very often, there was little or no work to do, and their apparent pride in their laziness was largely a matter of making a virtue, or a kind of grace, of necessity.

In Madrid he marvels at "the desire that men and women have of passing the time in each other's company... It appears not unlike madness to one who has long lived in England, where men of all ranks seem ashamed to hang long about the fair." Passing through Aragon he talks to a peasant, on his way to the shrine of the Virgen del Pilar at Saragossa, who condemns the government's attempts to reduce the number of religious festivals and pilgrimages as the meddling of atheistic foreigners. A priest from Sigüenza defends the Church's toleration, even encouragement, of "lascivious" dances: "Though often a little too free with regard to postures and gestures, they are still the most harmless diversion for our lower classes who, if they were forbidden, would find worse ways to amuse their evenings."

Nearing Barcelona, Baretti sees "Catalan rusticks toiling by moonlight in the fields," and learns that they work long hours to pay a punitive tax imposed for their "treachery" during the Spanish Succession war. And he notes that a new town—Barceloneta—is being built outside the medieval walls for an expanding textile trade ("many tailors, for the greater part of the cloathing for Spanish troops, in Spain and beyond sea, is made here").

Of Spanish inns he writes that "scarce one bed in ten is free from tormenting vermin" and that he could honestly commend only two establishments, one kept by a Frenchman, the other by an Italian. But any discomfort had been more than compensated by the chance to meet and talk to the people, to watch them dance the *fandango* and even to join in himself. Unlike Casanova, Baretti was loath to cross the Pyrenees. He knew he would miss the high spirits of the Spanish peasants: "Almost every creature in Spain can handle a guittar and the castanets and there is not one in a hundred but can shake his heels at the sound." Except in some Provencal villages, such jollity was unknown in France. Indeed Baretti comes close to Jardine's contrasting of French suavity ("they can caress you without affection, can flatter you without esteem") and Spanish plain speaking.

Major William Dalrymple's bluff, peppery journal records a five-month horseback ride which took him and a servant from the garrison in Gibraltar up to Galicia, braving many a tiresome ordeal in "a nation far behind the rest of Europe in improvements and conveniences. Except at La Carolina and for a few leagues about Madrid I have never seen any made roads." His only motive for the journey was, he says, curiosity; and this was keen enough to endure a customs search upon entering and leaving every town, the expense of a passport to cross provincial boundaries, and a series of "frontier taxes."

Andalusian inns were a trial: often there was "no bedding but straw." But on the bright side there was "a travelling pedlar from Seville, all urbanity and good humour. Every now and then he told us some facetious story, well larded with proverbs." If the summer heat was tiring, the natives' way of counteracting it could be disconcerting. In Cordoba, calling upon "people of consideration," he found them in heavily-shuttered lower rooms, "agreeably cool, though to an Englishman it was a very odd effect to enter a dark chamber where he must be some time before he can discover the person whom he visits." He thought the rigid formality of the *tertulia*, or evening At Home, where iced water was served with sugar-sticks and sweetmeats, very tedious; and he advises against taking literally the oft-repeated phrase of total hospitality, "My house is your house." The fact was that "if anything belonging to a Spaniard be praised, he immediately offers it with warmth, though nothing would disappoint him more than to accept it."

Baroque churches displeased him ("tawdry and overloaded with ornament"), and like Alexander Jardine, who describes Andalusia as "having for the most part a barren and naked appearance," Dalrymple was happy to move on. He preferred the plains of La

Mancha, where "everyone seemed to have a more sedate appearance," and noted with approval that "the Basques hold the Andalusians in contempt as being in immediate descent from the Moors." Beneath a scorching sun he rode on "through a country so flat that we had a horizon before us the same as at sea in a calm." At Aranjuez the leafy shade of the palace gardens was welcome, but he criticized the artificiality of "*parterres* where puerile devices are formed in myrtle borders, such as *fleurs de lis*, initial letters of names etc... A true taste for gardening has not reached this country."

After a glimpse of court circles he was even more critical of an aristocracy which had chosen "to reside slaves at Madrid... rendering themselves dependent on the prince by squandering their wealth, which should be spent on their estates to encourage the industry of their vassals." And as Labat had deplored the pauperizing effect of monastic hand-outs, so Dalrymple frowns on the misplaced charity of grandees who maintain a host of redundant pensioners and retainers, sometimes including a dwarfish buffoon ("the Duke of Alba's attends his master in the morning, and the instant he awakes is obliged to relate some facetious story to put his Grace in good humour").

An earlier English traveller had reported that in many Spanish inns the female servants supplemented their wages by prostitution. And the much-tried Major was convinced that this was no mere fabrication when, at a *posada* in Castile, he had to fight off the urgent importunities of a bedraggled kitchen wench. He may have been slightly mollified when at the naval port of El Ferrol he watched "fifteen prostitutes drummed out of town. They were placed on ladders carried upon men's shoulders, with the hair of their heads and eyebrows shaved off." Except for Santiago de Compostela, where "Ignorance daily crowds in superstitious votaries to contribute to the pleasures of the sacerdotal tribe," Dalrymple felt at home in Galicia. He appreciated the excellent beef and mutton, making special mention of Betanzos in this respect. And though the "barbarous music" of bagpipes and castanets jarred on him, he praised the enterprise of Galicians in trekking to Castile, to Portugal, and even to Andalusia for

Swinburne was the first writer to make known in England "the arts and monuments of the ancient inhabitants of Spain."

harvest and vintage. "Let us not say that all Spaniards are indolent when one sees such numbers wandering so far from home and labouring like slaves to obtain so poor a pittance. Yet, notwithstanding that the inhabitants of Castile depend on these people for their annual labour, they treat them as vagrants and hold them in the utmost contempt."

Unlike Dalrymple, most travellers of the time considered Andalusia a—if not *the*—high spot of their tour, though some were amazed by the casual neglect of architectural treasures. At Granada Henry Swinburne was shaken by the ruinous condition of the Alhambra and surprised that the governor, an invalid soldier, used his considerable leisure "not in profound speculations or learned researches, but in emptying as many bottles of wine as his only arm had steadiness to pour into his glass."

Richard Twiss, another rich young English tourist of the 1770s, thought it strange that in Cordoba "a great part of the furniture of the noblemen's houses was English, such as mahogany chairs and

Swinburne took a particular interest in Roman and
Moorish architecture.

tables, Wilton carpets etc." But he happily exchanged such Britannic
luxuries for the basic facilities of Andalusian *posadas* ("sleeping on
straw with our cloaths on was very convenient, for in the morning
having shaken off the straw and put on our hats, we were ready
dressed"). Indeed he states that "the first bugs I had yet felt in Spain"
were encountered in Gibraltar at an inn where he stayed after watching English officers "playing at golf on the sands."

Sir John Talbot Dillon, an Irishman who studied the physical
geography of Spain, was enraptured by the Valencian *huerta* and much
taken with the countryside around Málaga: "The dreary month of
January in a northern climate is here a source of delight; the fields are
full of perriwinkle, myrtle, oleander and lavender, with many other
flowers in full bloom." In Seville he was fascinated by the storks.
"Almost every tower is peopled with them and they return annually to
the same nests. They destroy all the vermin on the tops of the houses
and pick up a great number of snakes, so that they are welcome guests
and looked upon with peculiar veneration." Heading north, he found

that in Despeñaperros, a pass in the Sierra Morena notorious for robberies, a fancy toll had to be paid on "monkies, parrots, negroes, guittars unless played upon at the time, and married women unless in company with their husbands or producing certificates." Much of Castile, he says, is "bleak and dismal, with a great want of trees, to which the Castilians have such a dislike from the false notion that they increase the number of birds to eat up their corn: as if this reason would not hold good in other countries where shade is not so necessary to support the moisture of the soil."

Nor was this the only example of reckless improvidence. Crossing Extremadura en route to Lisbon in 1795, the young poet Robert Southey was aghast at the wreckage left by a royal progress. "His Most Catholic Majesty travels like a king of the Gypsies; his retinue, about 7,000 strong, strip the country without paying for anything, sleep in the woods, and burn down trees for fuel... Mules, horses and asses lie dead along the road... If the king has one solitary spark of humanity, he must be seriously grieved to behold the wretched state of his dominions. When the Moors possessed Extremadura this whole province was like a well-cultivated garden: at present the population is only 100,000 in a region 200 miles long and 60 wide."

Southey also noted that husbandry had been abandoned in favour of sheep ranges ("a slovenly and Tartar-like system of pasturage"). Some years later Lady Holland, travelling with her husband, two young sons, a tutor and the family doctor, reckoned that one of the greatest obstacles to progress was "the *mesta*, a code of laws which grants almost unlimited privileges to a company who possess the *merino* sheep... They prevent the purchase of land for tillage and their flocks range uncontrolled all over the kingdom." Equally lamentable was the number of people "either blind or almost so from violent inflammation of the eyelids, a disease very common in Spain and attributed to the smallpox." Inoculation, so successful in reducing the ravages of this scourge in Britain, had not, despite Joseph Baretti's urging, been attempted, perhaps because the Church condemned it as unnatural and therefore impious.

Travellers tended to have, or to develop, a special interest; and Augustus Fischer, a German tourist of the 1790s, set himself up as something of an authority on "the Spanish woman." "Her majestic step," he writes, "her sonorous voice, the vivacity of her gesticulation, indicate the temperature of her soul." But "the heating aliments that they use, and excess in their amusements, contribute to produce this effect—at forty a Spanish woman seems twice as old... Almost all have a down of hair on their upper lip, a peculiarity which shows the warmth of their constitutions, but which is so disagreeable that they have recourse to *velleras* whose business it is to pluck out the hair. Most have spoiled their teeth by the immoderate use of sweetmeats and often become very stout, a type to which the Spaniards themselves apply the term *jamonas.*"

Fischer quotes a saying that "the women of Biscay are industrious, those of Catalonia good housewives, those of Castile prudes, those of Andalusia ardent, those of Valencia clean, and *those of my own province the most desirable,*" but he concludes that climate is a vital factor.

"The fire of the northern Spaniards changes in the south into a devouring flame," and nowhere more so than in Cadiz. There "the beauty of the Andalusian women, their exalted fanaticism" reached the highest, most frantic pitch, especially "when the *solano* blows, for then the very air they breathe is on fire and the sexes seek each other with equal eagerness."

On Lord Byron too, briefly visiting Andalusia in 1809, Cadiz left an impression of simmering lust—the perfect place for a Romantic rake on a sex safari. "The most delightful town I ever beheld," he wrote to his mother, "full of the fairest women in Spain, the Cadiz belles being the Lancashire witches of the land."

Richard Twiss, though charmed, during the *paseo* at Cadiz, to observe "several ladies who had fixed glowworms to their hair, which had a luxurious and pleasing effect," disapproved of women who "would either faint, or feign to faint, at the sight of a frog, a spider etc" but revelled in the bullfight, "a spectacle exhibiting every species of cruelty: the greater the barbarity and the more the bloodshed, the greater enjoyment they testify, clapping their hands, waving their handkerchiefs, and hallooing the more to enrage the bull. I have seen some women throw handfuls of nuts into the arena of combat in hopes of causing the men who fight the bull on foot to fall over them."

Though less concerned with the behaviour of female spectators, other writers expressed their opinion of "bullfeasts." Swinburne and Jardine regretted the days when this had been the sport of noble amateurs, now alas replaced by "hired gladiators who are generally butchers by profession." Casanova dismissed bullfighting as "most barbarous and likely to have a bad effect on national morals." The Rev Joseph Townsend, writing in the 1780s, showed himself to be something of an *aficionado*—bulls, he explains, are "*claro*, that is impetuous and without disguise," or "*obscuro*, that is circumspect or crafty." And the Rev Clarke went so far as to call a slap-up royal fiesta "one of the finest spectacles in the world." Why, he asked, should Spaniards be condemned for enjoying it when "my own country is bigotted to its customs of bull-baiting, cockfighting etc. I do not deny that the *corrida* will not bear the speculations of the closet or the compassionate feelings of a tender heart. But after all one must not speculate too nicely lest we should lose the hardness of manhood in the softer sentiments of philosophy."

But if these Anglican clerics refused to be censorious (Townsend reserved his thunders for Spanish roads), the son of a Norfolk parson was perhaps the first Briton openly to show moral indignation. After attending a *fiesta de toros* in Cadiz in 1793 Horatio Nelson exclaimed that the disembowelling of five horses had sickened him; that the goring of two *toreros* had seemed like poetic justice; and that the bloodthirstiness of the spectators had made him feel that "he would not have been displeased to see them tossed." Bourgoing was convinced that only the abolition of those twin barbarisms, the *corrida* and the Inquisition, would open the way to progress, and Lady Holland echoed Nelson's sentiments, declaring that "from the bottom of my heart did I cry "*Viva toro!*" when a man was thrown down by a

Byron—in *Childe Harold's Pilgramage* gave his relfections on a bullfight:
"Such the ungentle sport that oft invites/The Spanish maid and cheers
the Spanish swain/Nurtured in blood betimes, his heart delights/
In vengeance, gloating on another's pain."

bull. The only relief to my feelings is that eight or ten *toreros* have been
killed within these few years in Andalusia, and many elsewhere."

Faced with a nation so abruptly plunged from imperial glory
into terrible, if picturesque, decay, writers were bound to seek reasons
and to hazard generalizations. "We strangers and sojourners here,"
wrote Jardine, "are very apt to think we could easily improve this
country—hence perhaps arises the proverbial saying To *build castles in
Spain.*" Emphasizing the influence of natural barriers such as mountain chains and rivers on linguistic and cultural differences, he argued
that centralized rule was not only unworkable but psychologically
harmful. Interminable delays and local resistance to decrees issuing
from Madrid had created chaos, cynicism and a tribal brand of *individualismo*. "Each must live perpetually on his guard as if surrounded
by enemies. Hence the value and frequent use for private friendships—
hence too the frequent assassinations."

Dalrymple was inclined to explain Spanish reserve by fear of the Inquisition, "employing its familiars in every part of the realm, which urged them to have a curb on their tongues." But such unnatural restraint inevitably resulted in sudden outbursts of passion ("Spaniards are revengeful and stabbing still prevails"). Yet "the malignant blasts of despotism" were, he thought, tempered by a certain quasi-democratic sense of equality in the sight of God. "The people throughout are free from diffidence... Each man appears to have a conscious dignity which is not so conspicuous in other parts of the world. If even a beggar asks alms and it be not granted, the supplicant is refused in the most compassionate tones... Insult is never added to misfortune."

To the Rev. Clarke the "blind bigotry" of the Church was evident in a thoughtless reverence for tradition which had not only emasculated education but affected decisions in every sphere, as when the Council of Castile rejected a scheme to make the Tagus navigable to Lisbon by joining it to the Manzanares at Madrid on the grounds that "if it had pleased God that these two rivers should be joined, He would not have wanted human assistance... To attempt it, therefore, would be to violate the decrees of His providence."

Indeed, said Jardine, in priest-ridden communities one had to use the system. Thefts from his house in La Coruña were frequent, but the best hope of recovering stolen goods was "to apply to the Father Confessor, who often brings them to you on condition of no questions being asked." Similarly, he reasoned that since Spain was so fragmented (Bourgoing described it as an uneasy federation with strong regional differences) why not work with the grain? Why not encourage local enterprise and with it the emergence of a substantial capitalist middle class so vital to any real economic surge? "The people must be invited to cooperate, given a sense of their importance," instead of being crushed by taxes to finance projects conceived by distant bureaucrats. Jardine instances the relatively good roads in the Basque provinces ("the last asylum of liberty in Spain"), built by local initiative, as a token of what could be achieved.

Captured by the British in 1704 Gibraltar, soon to become a noted
smuggling centre, withstood several sieges. But the Frenchman Pbre Labat
reported that ragged, unpaid Spanish troops were more likely to turn
bandit or smuggler than to fight the official foe.

Only along the sea-shore, "like a lace set round an old threadbare coat," had contact with the outside world prevented the fatalistic
lethargy, veneered with "ennobling" pride, noted by Swinburne.
"Thousands of men in all parts of the realm pass their whole day
wrapped up in a cloak, standing in rows against a wall or dozing under
a tree... I have heard a peasant refuse to run an errand because he had
that morning earned as much already as would last him the day
without putting himself to further trouble."

Bourgoing adroitly side-stepped the problem of "national
character" by observing that "we must subdivide Spaniards into
Castilians, Catalans, Aragonese, Navarrese, Andalusians, Biscayans and
Asturians, and draw of each of these peoples a separate portrait: a task
difficult and unpleasant, and which could not be accomplished
without accompanying every rule with an exception." But he too
noticed that wherever industry was stimulated and there was "a facility
of conveyance," as at Barcelona and Valencia and in the Basque
provinces, there was plenty of bustle. Elsewhere the lack of passable

roads, canals and navigable rivers made transport slow and expensive. When in the 1770s Madrid had been short of food the government had been forced "to assemble, from all parts, no less than 30,000 draft animals." Poor communications put Spain "at the mercy of foreigners even when some of her provinces are provided in abundance." For example, "the kingdom of Valencia procures corn principally from Italy and Barbary. That which she gets from La Mancha is dearer because it can only be conveyed by mules." Government was further hampered by the Moorish habit of florid verbosity, "one of the main causes of the lack of clear reasoning" which lay behind the refusal to come to terms with obvious if unpalatable realities. Though the days of imperial splendour were gone, "the pretensions for which it formed an excuse have survived. The mask remains. Hence that proud and grave exterior which distinguishes the Spaniard still."

Baretti, taking a longer view, suggested that since every empire had gone through a rise-and-fall-cycle, there was no reason to suppose that Spain's successful rivals would escape it. He foresaw a time when currently top-dog England would be overtaken, thus "entitling the fashionable characterizers of the next generations to brand their unborn progeny with that same note of idleness which they have at present some right to bestow on other nations, the Spanish in particular."

Meanwhile, as Jardine realized, foreign visitors were likely to be torn between a desire to "improve" Spain and a fancy for its romantic-archaic backwardness. They could feel superior, or wallow in antiquarian nostalgia, or both. And armed with guide-bookish data they were coming in a steadily growing trickle.

For the serious traveller Jardine recommends a knowledge and love of one's own country; a fixed base, so as to combine residence with exploration; female company; and at least two extensive tours. Baretti advised tourists to keep luggage to a minimum and above all to take a sleeping-bag. Clarke stresses the need to "carry your provisions and bedding with you" and cautions that the going will often be tough, as in Leon ("a naked, dreadful, barren rock, a brown horror").

Barreti includes an appendix with a stage-by-stage itinerary.

Swinburne offers a note on currency exchange and a careful inn-rating ("Venta del Platero, as bad as any in Spain... Cartagena, Aguila d'Oro, excellent... Cadiz, Caballo Blanco, Italian"). Spanish cuisine receives attention too. Baretti supplies a recipe "to dress Arroz a la Valencia." Twiss, recording his arrival at a village near Algerciras which had no inn or venta, says he "prevailed on an old woman to let me pass the night on a large chest in her shop" and supped on *gazpacho*. This, he writes, is an excellent kind of *soupe-maigre*, than which nothing can be more refreshing during the violant heats; it is made by putting a sufficient quantity of oil, vinegar, salt and pepper into a quart of cold water and adding to it crusts of bread, garlick and onions shred small." "Our hostess," he adds, "supplied us with plenty of fruit and then obligingly smoked a *segar* with me."

Such zest and homely detail brought Spain into sharp, beguiling focus, and at the end of the century Augustus Fischer acknowledged the role of British writers in changing attitudes. No longer was a journey in Spain "considered an expedition to a country of savages nearly on a par with the Hottentots." Clearly anticipating a rush of leisurely explorers to this newly-promoted destination, Fischer advised them to peregrinate from April to October. For then, moving from north to south, they would "gradually accustom themselves to the climate; and if during the hot months you travel in the old Spanish manner in the mornings and evenings, you will suffer but little from the heat and will enjoy all the pleasures the country affords during the best seasons of the year."

But just as a tourist surge began to gather momentum, the Peninsular War broke out. From 1808 to 1814 soldiers of many nations were the involuntary, far from popular, and often far from complimentary, tourists.

III

TROUBLED TIMES

The Peninsular War and Carlist rebellion

Fitful attempts at modernization had deeply antagonized the "Black Spain" that combined a reactionary Church, a feudal aristocracy, and xenophobic masses. Many Spanish progressives, tired of the seemingly hopeless struggle against *costumbrismo*, began to see revolutionary France as a potential saviour.

Such were the *afrancesados* who welcomed the imposition of Napoleon's brother Joseph Bonaparte as king in 1808. At last perhaps an Age of Reason would dawn and the Inquisition be abolished (it was, and two-thirds of the convents were closed). Black Spain rapidly if chaotically mobilized against such heresy and, with the help of Anglo-Portuguese forces led first by Sir John Moore and then by Sir Arthur Wellesley (later Duke of Wellington), prepared for a "war of independence."

As Moore and Wellington soon discovered, "national resistance" was a myth. Provincial juntas ignored the so-called Supreme junta and squabbled among themselves (Seville almost declared war on Granada). In both Spains, *afrancesado* and "patriotic," there was a constant fear that the "black rabble" would launch a murderous war of their own on the rich. "Patriotic" liberals, themselves much influenced by French political theory, were, in their last refuge—the constituent Cortes at Cadiz—outnumbered by reactionaries and representatives of the American colonies, poised to make their bids for independence.

Not surprisingly, foreigners caught up in this complex turmoil were baffled and exasperated.

Outnumbered and, in snow and icy sleet, closely pursued in the long retreat to La Coruña and Vigo of December 1808, the British army was pushed to the limits of endurance. In the *Recollections of Rifleman Harris*, the author describes how exhausted, starving, bare-foot soldiers threw away their weapons and heavy packs and "linked arm in arm to support each other, like a party of drunkards." Having dragged himself up a lane to a hovel where, watched by gloomy Galician peasants, he devoured "some coarse black bread and a pitcher of sour wine," Harris forced himself to stay awake. "Knowing the treachery of the Spanish character, I refused to relinquish possession of my rifle, and my right hand was ready in an instant to unsheathe my bayonet."

His resentment at the "treachery" of Spaniards—an accusation which they retorted on their "cowardly" allies—was shared by British commanders.

"If our army were in enemy country," reported Sir John Moore, "it could not be more completely left to itself... The people run away, the villages are deserted." Despising party politics, Wellington had no patience with bickering juntas and liberal "windbags." His letters and dispatches bristled with fury, as when he defined "the national disease" as "boasting of the strength and power of Spain... then sitting down quietly and indulging their national indolence." Spaniards, he complains, "cry *viva*! and swear that my mother is a saint and are very fond of us and hate the French; but they are, in general, the most incapable of useful exertion of all the nations I have ever known; the most vain and the most ignorant... It really appears as if they were all drunk and thinking and talking of any other subject but Spain."

Finally, in a phrase quoted in 1936 by Anthony Eden to justify non-intervention in what he called "the War of the Spanish Obsession," Wellington remarked that "jealousy of the interference of foreigners in their internal concerns is the characteristic of all Spaniards."

Strategically sited on the Portuguese frontier, Badajoz was several times besieged during the Peninsular War.

But though contemptuous of the regular Spanish armies ("I cannot say that the officers do anything as it ought to be done, with the exception of running away"), he praised the usefulness of guerrilla bands, especially when trained by British officers. The more efficient ones, he might have added, for as Major the Hon. Charles Cocks, a keen young protégé of the Iron Duke, noted, too many were wealthy fops who had bought their commissions and refused to take soldiering seriously for fear of behaving like mere tradesmen.

Cocks had taken the trouble to learn Spanish and was angered by the stupidity of some of his colleagues. "Can you," he wrote to his sister, "imagine a Gentleman reporting officially that the French army had gone to Castile, which he conceived must be a very large town, for it held the whole army?" He did not share the contempt for Spain which he heard all round him ("I am not inclined to such spiteful sentiments. I see so many remains of a great and noble people and have received so many personal kindnesses"); and in doggerel verse he tried to convey the fun of dances held in village barns or inns:

We get 18 or 20 girls, good ones and bad ones,
And we all fall a-capering like so many mad ones,
The rooms here are never boarded and are mostly of clay,
So you may easily conceive what a dust flies in every
way...
You must plainly understand we've no senhoras or splashers
For the little villages we're in don't boast such grand dashers.
Ours are honest peasant girls who make pork sausages all day
And at night divert themselves in their own quiet way.
When we sit down some of the natives come forth,
They always sing and dance together as a matter of course.
Their instruments are only a key and a pewter platter, It's no
great music but it makes the devil of a clatter,
And they keep such time to their fandangoes and Malbrook
That faith, they sometimes jig till the very walls have shook...

When Wellington was appointed Generalisimo, Cocks hoped that Spanish troops "drilled by us and mingled with us" would become more disciplined and effective. But he had his doubts. "There will never be any want of guerrillas, for a Spaniard is very vain and fond of an irregular plundering life: he does not care for hardships in the least, but cannot bear continual labour."

Major-General Lord Blayney, an Irish peer captured in October 1810 when an expeditionary force led by him was routed after landing at Fuengirola, spent the next three months travelling across Spain as a very privileged prisoner of war ("Owing to my acquaintance with many of the ancient French *noblesse*, I found myself perfectly at ease with General Sebastiani's staff). At Granada, where British and German prisoners, penned in part of the Alhambra, rioted, Blayney, a man of culture, criticized Sebastiani for "fitting up some of the apartments in the modern style: no proof of his good taste, for a Parisian salon or boudoir in a Moorish palace 500 years old is almost as absurd as dressing an antique statue in the costume of a modern *petit maitre*." When Sebastiani, viewing some gem-studded ecclesiastical treasures, pitied the poor Spaniards who had toiled to provide them, Blayney reflected that "if plundering the churches was for the good of the country, the French had taken a most lively interest in its welfare." But he agreed that one desirable result of the French regime was the eviction of "hordes of drone-like monks and nuns."

That revolution was soon to be reversed. Returning from house-arrest in France, King Ferdinand VII could not prevent a reactionary backlash of the *apostólicos* (clerical traditionalists) which annulled the liberal constitution drafted by the Cadiz Cortes, restored the Jesuits and the Inquisition, founded a Society of the Exterminating Angel, and drove thousands of *afrancesados* (collaborators) into exile. Undeterred by this heavily-charged atmosphere, George Ticknor, an earnest and scholarly young Bostonian, arrived in May 1818 for a six-month stay as part of a leisurely Grand Tour, the first of three Americans who gave their impressions of Spain in this period of vengeful extremism.

The 400-mile, 13-day coach journey from Barcelona to Madrid was a severe ordeal. "Travelling from 4 o'clock in the morning until 7 at night would not bring us forward more than 22 miles... I have not been in a single inn where the lower storey was not a stable and the upper one as full of fleas as if it were under an Egyptian curse... Not once have I taken off my clothes except to change them, and in Madrid I find myself in quarters little more decent." Yet, he adds, "I never made a gayer journey in my life," thanks to the "hearty kindness" of Spanish fellow-travellers and lively discussions about *Don Quixote*, which Ticknor read aloud to the company ("it was a pleasure to see the effect this extraordinary book produces on the people from whose very blood and character it is drawn").

Madrid, where the mob, in xenophobic ecstasy, had greeted the king's restoration with the cry of "Long live our chains!", he thought "far from handsome... dead animals are not uncommon in the

Though showered with gifts and honours for his part in ending the
French occupation, the "Iron" Duke of Wellington irritably remarked
that Spaniards were "the most incapable of useful exertion of
all the nations I have ever known."

streets." Hospitals were frighteningly unhygienic and ill-equipped,
schools and theatres stifled by the Inquisition. Ferdinand VII was "a
vulgar blackguard," government "such a confusion of abuses as never
existed before since society was organized." Bribery was rampant, royal
decrees incessant but largely ignored.

Yet in this land of paradox Ticknor got the impression that a
zany balance had been precariously achieved. "There's a kind of tacit
compromise that the king shall issue decrees and that the people shall
be tolerated in disobedience; and in this way disturbances are avoided.
If however the king should attempt to execute even one half of
the decrees that are nominally in force he would raise a rebellion in a
fortnight."

He could not decide whether the dreariness of middle class
Spaniards, "the most reserved of all the population," was due to lack of
culture or to fear of speaking freely in "that portion of the people

Even when war did not interfere, travel was something of a campaign
in itself. Alexandre Dumas grumbled that "even if the coach does not capsize,
it bounces high in the air at least twice before it can
settle on all four wheels again."

which has always been most obnoxious to despots and inquisitors."
Whatever the reason, it was much more fun to mingle with the masses,
for "though the surface of the ocean be everywhere vexed, its depths
remain tranquil and undisturbed." Watching peasants at work he
noted: "At the gates of Madrid, just such a threshing floor as is
described in the Old Testament... the Romans used when they were
here, for I have it on a coin of Caesar Augustus." For Ticknor as for
subsequent Hispanophiles, including Gerald Brenan and Robert
Graves, such archaic scenes had a powerful romantic appeal.

"Spain and the Spanish people," he said, "amuse me more than
anything I have met in Europe. There is more originality in the
popular manners and feelings, more force without barbarism, than I
have found anywhere else... In all that relates to manners Cervantes
and Le Sage are historians. When you have crossed the Pyrenees you
have not only passed from one country and climate to another, you

have gone back a couple of centuries in your chronology."

And if the Italians were the most musical people, "Spaniards of all classes, but particularly the lowest" were fondest of dancing. "Every evening as I come home I find little groups of them dancing the *bolero*, the *fandango* and the *manchegas* in the streets... Their very movements seem from nature to be graceful and their resting positions picturesque." Sometimes, too, returning from an embassy ball or reception, he would "find a lover with his guitar before the house of his mistress, singing his passion and suffering."

Ever industrious, Ticknor made a "large collection of these *seguidillas*," and faithfully recorded his reaction to a picturesque survival of which he did not approve: the bullfight. After forcing himself to attend two *corridas* he wrote that "the horrid sights I witnessed completely unmanned me. The first time I was carried out by one of the guards, the second time I was barely able to get out alone."

But he realized that these saturnalian orgies could be regarded as useful safety-valves, rather as today sociologists argue that gang warfare, if driven from the terraces at football matches, will erupt in the streets. "The masses feel their own strength, they enter into the rights of their own importance and power. Their exclamations often seem revolutionary... Of one bull, who shrank from the contest, several young men kept shouting that he was as cowardly as the king." Perfervid fans were more likely to murder each other than to set about their oppressors. "Before my very eyes," said Ticknor, "a man stabbed his brother, who fell dead in the street, in consequence of a difference that had arisen in the amphitheatre."

He selected as a trait common to most Spaniards "an instinctive uprightness which prevents them from servility." Never had he seen such unservile domestics, "joining in the conversation at the Duchess of Osuna's, for instance, while they wait at table."

Madrid had been an education in itself, but Ticknor's Spanish sojourn reached a lyrical climax when he travelled south in the fall. "The Castilians," he says (and to forestall any giggles, by "gay" he means "sociable"), "are gay in their private circles; the Andalusians are gay always and everywhere, and they have an open-heartedness towards strangers which is much more fascinating."

The shadow of the Inquisition seemed even darker in the brilliant sunlight and Moorish setting of Granada, where "a printed decree was posted up condemning anew the heresy of Martin Luther and calling upon servants to denounce their masters, children their parents, wives their husbands, etc." How heavenly it was, by comparison, to explore the airy heights of the Alhambra, half fortress half pleasure palace, which inspired this sober student (who became a respected and highly respectable Hispanist) to one of the first really full-blooded tourist rhapsodies. The very ruinousness, he thought, intensified a mysterious charm that ravished the senses with the sound of fountains and gurgling water channels. Contrasting the "light, luxurious style of Arabian architecture" with "the gloomy grandeur of the North," he ringingly announced that "the Alhambra is a name which will make my blood thrill if I live to the frosts of a century... a riotous, tumultuous pleasure like a kind of sensual enjoyment."

Thoroughly beglamoured, Ticknor felt the romantic tourist's longing to experience, however briefly, a way of life utterly remote from his normal routine; and once again Andalusia came up trumps. Aiming to travel to Lisbon from Seville he was told that the best route, which passed through Badajoz, was "so dangerous from the number of robbers, that I resolved to go directly across the mountains under the protection of one of the regular bodies of contrabandists that smuggle dollars from Seville to Lisbon and in return smuggle back English goods from Lisbon to Seville." He found the smugglers, 28 of them with 40 mules, "high-spirited, high-minded fellows" with not a hint of criminal stealth about them." Each was "armed with a gun, a pair of pistols, a sword and a dirk." Ticknor enjoyed a glorious dude vagabond week, "sleeping out every night but one, dining under trees at noon." Time then to "say farewell to the only country in the world, perhaps, where I could have led such a life; the only one indeed where it would have been safer to be under the protection of outlaws than under that of the government against which they array themselves."

Smugglers (*contrabandistas*), used to travelling rough, flourished in the wake of war. According to Richard Ford smuggling was "the only well-organised commercial system". Washington Irving saw "open-handed contrabandistas" as "a kind of mongrel chivalry."

In 1829 when another, more celebrated American, the diplomat Washington Irving, journeyed to Andalusia from Madrid, Spain was still chronically unstable. A Liberal revolt followed by a spell of radical rule and a "Red" terror had ended, barely ten years after the defeat of Napoleon, when French armies were called in to restore order. A second, even more ferocious, "Black" terror had caused another exodus of refugees, including 80-year-old Francisco Goya, whose gloomy paintings expressed his despair at the triumph of reaction. Banditry and smuggling, closely allied and firmly established as symbols of wild, romantic Spain, flourished. Indeed, in a passage deleted from his *Handbook for Travellers in Spain*, Richard Ford was to describe smuggling as "the only rich, active and well-organized commercial system."

Riding in a landscape which "partook of the stern and solitary character of Africa," Washington Irving was struck by "the absence of singing birds, a natural consequence of the want of groves and hedges," and by hill-top or crag-top villages "with mouldering battlements and ruined watch-tower" originally built to resist Moorish border raids, but now useful for protection against "the maraudings of roving freebooters." Few people ventured abroad without a gun, and even short journeys were "undertaken with the preparation of a warlike enterprise... The carriers congregate in convoys and set off in large and well-armed trains."

Gibraltar had long been notorious as a smuggling centre. Coastal patrols, bribed or misled by false information, were largely ineffectual. Bandits set up as smugglers when they had accumulated sufficient capital, and Irving attributed "the galliard character" of so many Andalusians to the excitement, profits and social prestige of their trade. Moving mostly at night, gangs would by day "lie quiet in gullies or in lonely farmhouses, where they are generally well-received... Much of the finery and trinkets worn by the wives and daughters of the mountain hamlets are presents from open-handed *contrabandistas...* a kind of mongrel chivalry."

But the behaviour of petty bandits, or sierra muggers, could be distinctly unpleasant. Having, at an inn at Loja, seen the fate of two Asturian pedlars, "stripped of their money, beaten for having offered resistance, and left almost naked," Irving advised travellers to take "a little surplus of hard dollars by way of a robber purse to satisfy the gentlemen of the road."

Henry Inglis, a Scottish writer who toured Spain in 1830, described the bandit industry in its wider ramifications. Security precautions were impressive. Leaving Barcelona in a mail coach, Inglis counted "three carabines, four cases of pistols, and three additional guards each with a long sabre... There is undoubtedly some exaggeration about the robbery of public conveyances, but the mails are occasionally stopped in the southern parts." In a show of firmness the government had actually refused to "enter into a treaty with banditti for the safety of the mails; and as resistance must be made in case of attack, the traveller by mail is necessarily placed in a dangerous position." In a stage coach however there was "comparatively little risk. Every one of the principal diligences pays black mail to the banditti for their protection." A spokesman had guaranteed that there would be no problems with "robbers of consequence" on the Madrid-Seville run, but stressed that they could not be responsible for small fry (*ladrones de ninguna consideración*). Recently a diligence had been held up by "unofficial" operators, so a new arrangement had been made. "One of the chiefs accompanies the coach on its journey and overawes by his presence the robbers of inferior degree."

In Seville, says Inglis, religion and smuggling were closely linked, there being "several convents on the outskirts of the city, and in particular a nunnery, active as depots for smuggled goods and of course keeping a liberal share of the profits." Morals were "at the lowest possible ebb," "the worst example being set by the churchmen. It is a common saying in Seville that the reason why one sees so few pretty women in the street is that they are all in the houses of the clergy." There was too a story that the archbishop, having run into debt, had asked the king for advice and did not scruple to obey the royal suggestion: "'Do as I do and pay nobody.'"

The lower classes were "less abstemious" than in Castile and much addicted to gambling. Inglis claims to have visited a hospital "dedicated to the sole purpose of receiving wounded persons" and to have ascertained that "during the past fourteen days twentyone people had been taken in with stab wounds. They would not inform me how many of them died."

Málaga was hardly more edifying. "A Spanish lady married to a highly respectable Scotch merchant told me that she did not know one Spanish woman who had always led a virtuous life." Then there was "the great laxity of female conversation. I was informed by the English mother of three grown-up daughters that it was impossible to allow them to keep company with either married or unmarried Spanish women; and this I can very well believe, judging by the tone of conversation to which I myself have been witness."

Inglis gives no examples, but experience of Andalusian ventas

After slow and hazardous coach journeys, inns were an ordeal. "I have not
been in a single one", said the young American George Ticknor, "where the
lower storey was not a stable and the upper as full of fleas
as if it were under an Egyptian curse."

(wayside inns) no doubt helped to sharpen his Presbyterian strictures.
Flea-bites and the noise of mules stamping and tinkling their bells "prevented the gentle approaches of sleep," while unglazed windows
admitting blasts of wind and rain completed his discomfiture. Contrary
to popular belief, winter days in southern Spain could be cold to a degree
which "in England would be thought to demand closed windows and a
blazing fire." Going to seek his tartana (light covered carriage) after a
restless night in one posada he found "no fewer than 69 mules in the
house, the muleteers sleeping beside them. All were going to Granada,
laden with the Esparto rush which is manufactured into baskets."

Toledo he thought "intensely Spanish... Men of all ranks wear the cloak and the small, round, high crowned hat. Among women black is the universal dress and scarcely any enters a church unveiled." The Plaza Real swarmed with clergy: "canons, prebendaries, curates, and twenty different orders of friars are seen standing in groups, strolling under the piazzas or seated upon benches, refreshing themselves with melons or grapes. There cannot be a more perfect realization of "fat, contented ignorance" than the Plaza presents every day after dinner."

Hoping for a livelier social scene in Madrid, Inglis was sadly disappointed. At court foreigners were regarded with suspicion, diplomats were treated as "little different from spies," and all together there was "nothing like gaiety in the upper ranks of the metropolis." A British consul had depressed him by revealing that after four years in Spain "he did not know if the Spaniards dined off a tablecloth" and that he would be surprised if he ever saw the inside of a Spanish house. The British ambassador admitted that he "knew nobody and visited nowhere." So-called newspapers were full of "royal ordinances breathing vengeance against those who desire to return from exile or declaring that the universities shall be closed and education suspended"; and there were many items about ecclesiastical trivia. But "not a syllable commenting on decrees that deal out injustice or strangle improvement," so that the astonished visitor "says within himself, this is the most wonderful country under the sun, for here intellect wields no power."

The best entertainment was the Sunday evening paseo when "the whole population passes down the Calle de Alcala to the Prado." Inglis scrutinized the throng carefully with the object of deciding whether "the belief in the witchery of Spanish women which obtains very general credence in England" had any validity. His answer was no—and yes. No, because there was "not one strikingly lovely countenance, no fine skin, no glossy hair. Dark, expressive eyes I certainly did see, but they were generally too ill-supported to produce much effect." Yes, because he had never seen women walk so beguilingly or carry themselves so gracefully, "one hand holding the folds of the mantilla just below the waist, the other inclined upward, wielding, with an effect the most miraculous, that mysterious instrument the fan, whose powers are nowhere to be seen displayed to such advantage as on the Prado, where it is a substitute for speech and an interpreter of etiquette."

On bullfights too Inglis' attitude was ambivalent, or perhaps partly tailored for a British readership. The spectacle had "a character of barbarism and cruelty sufficient to separate Spain from the list of civilized nations." Yet it was nevertheless "one of so stirring and extraordinary a kind that I think it would almost repay a journey to Madrid, even if the traveller set off next morning on his return."

But his general conclusions were sombre. "Too often," he writes, "the mass of Spaniards take little heed of the vices of the government." Except perhaps in the Basque provinces, it was "a matter of indifference whether Spain be ruled by a Calligula or Titcus... The total ignorance of the uses and nature of political freedom will yet, for many years prove a barrier to the progress of free institutions in the Peninsula." This was particularly true, he thought, of the Spaniard of the southern provinces; "give him his shade in summer and his sunshine in winter; his tobacco, his melon, his dates, his bread, his wine, and a hole to creep into, and he asks no more."

The Carlist War which began soon after the death of Ferdinand VII in 1833 lined up the supporters of his brother Don Carlos—the choice of Black Spain—against "Cristinos" who backed the "liberal" regime of the Regent Maria Cristina. The main Carlist strength was among Basque, especially Navarrese, peasants determined to retain or regain their ancient fueros. An ill-equipped, hastily recruited British Auxiliary Legion spent two miserable years in the Basque country fighting (or more often dying of typhus in scabby winter quarters) for the liberal cause. No more welcome than Wellington's "scum of the earth," the legionaries were seldom paid their wages, were shaken by the atrocities committed by both sides, and when they did get into action were usually outmanoeuvred by Carlist guerrillas in hilly terrain.

In Madrid the delighted Ticknor often watched "little groups dancing
the bolero, the fandango and the manchegas in the streets", and reckoned
that "when you have crossed the Pyrenees ... you have gone back a
couple of centuries in your chronology."

An English officer described his amazement at the Carlists'
bravado in battle: "Many would caper and dance *fandango* on the tops
of the breastworks, with balls and shells flying on all sides... They
would clap their buttocks in derision as the guns fired, waving their
caps and black flags and shouting "Down with the Queen! Carlos for
ever!" His summary of an inglorious experience was even more viru-
lent than that of Moore or of Wellington. "Thousands of Britons have
been sacrificed in the defence of a disgraceful cause for a set of treacherous Spaniards" whose friendship was "fickle as the wind; and once
offended their hatred is never satiated until they have imbrued their
knife in the blood of their victim. They are bigoted in their religion
and opinions, considering no one equal to themselves... Yet there is
scarcely one in 300 who can read or write his name."

The standard of literacy in the British Legion was probably not
much higher. And Slidell Mackenzie's account of Spain in 1834 bears

out George Borrow's assertion that most Spaniards, used as they were to lethal civil commotion, took little interest in the Carlist fracas, which was largely confined to the northern regions. A dashing young American naval officer who had been banned by royal edict from entering the country because of a previous book which contained injurious expressions concerning the king and the royal family of Spain and sacrilegious mockery of her institutions and laws," Mackenzie had no difficulty crossing the Pyrenees with one of the many Basque smuggler-couriers whose business was booming. In Pamplona Sylveti Fermin (the muleteer) and an innkeeper did not talk about the war but about smoking. "'How is it,'" asked the posadero, "that you throw your smoke away? You should swallow it all, man... One cigar does me more good that way than a dozen drawn in and puffed out again." Sylveti responded and a learned argument took place in which the relative qualities of Brazilian, Cuban and American tobacco were duly characterized and compared."

From Pamplona, Mackenzie travelled with another *contrabandista*, the roguish Ramón, very *majo* in Andalusian gear: "light green velvet jacket and breeches adorned with buttons... leather leggings and gacho hat well garnished with beads and riband. A yellow handkerchief round his neck confined by a huge silver ring set with bits of shiny glass... Abundant knife-cuts on his face and hands." A tough, fast-talking character, he saw them safely through a series of ventas of ill repute; one, says Mackenzie, having a Sweeney Todd reputation. He noticed that, compared with Navarre, the inns and roads in Aragon were wretched, since the province was administered from Madrid, which "instead of watching over the interests of the Aragonese, lavishes their money on courtesans or spends it on soldiers for their subjugation."

Ramón confided that his current enterprise was the smuggling of rams' horns from Navarre to the cutlers of Zaragoza who would turn them into knife handles. He also had in his cart "a quantity of horn combs such as are worn by women, which though of such universal use in Spain are all manufactured in foreign countries." He welcomed the Carlist rebellion because, he maintained, the armies "consumed goods and kept the people employed." A tailor by trade, Ramón was a close student of fashions: " "Look at an English coat or an English hat," he cried, "and tell me whether England be not the greatest nation!"

Going on to Madrid by coach, Mackenzie found the Puerta del Sol, "where eight streets meet," much as on his earlier visit. "The same collection of idle loungers enveloped in their cloaks... The shed of the man who sold the tickets of the hog lottery, while beside him lay apparently the same hog, black and glossy." Madrid being the liberal-Cristino headquarters, theatres were featuring satires on priestcraft and "the absurd folly of becoming a nun." But it was disconcerting to see that some citizens were "rapidly becoming Frenchified. A few women have already adopted the bonnet on the Prado instead of the mantilla. Men have substituted a stiff, ungainly surtout for the toga-like and convenient capa." Nor had "the delightful national airs, so full of feeling and gaiety" escaped revision, "replaced by foreign ones or else the music of the bolero and the cachucha so perverted as to be no longer recognizable." There was even a tendency "to graft on to dances pirouettes and feats of agility wholly unsuited to their easy style and voluptuous languor."

If this was the style of the progressive future, is was hard not to feel sympathy with those intensely conservative peasants who preferred an old-fashioned Carlist despotism, that would confirm their progress-obstructing *fueros*, to "the tyranny of a thousand bourgeois."

IV

ROMANTIC SPAIN

From Carmen to the Alhambra

"My dear Sarah... This is the country for a national novelist," wrote the 26-year-old Benjamin Disraeli in a wish-you-were-here letter to his sister posted during a two-month tour of Andalusia in summer 1830. "The alfresco life of the inhabitants induces a variety of the most picturesque manners, their semi-savageness making each district retain with barbarous jealousy their own customs and their own costumes. A weak government resolves society into its original elements and robbery becomes more honourable than war, inasmuch as the robber is paid, the soldier in arrear... Oh! Wonderful Spain! Think of this romantic land covered with Moorish ruins and full of Murillo! Ah that I could describe to you the wonders of the painted temples of Seville, ah that I could wander with you amid the fantastic and imaginative walls of delicate Alhambra!... I thought that enthusiasm was dead within me and nothing could be new... I dare to say that I am better. It is all the Sun."

Disraeli, an Anglicized Jew and future Prime Minister (but in 1830 an aspiring young writer), visited Andalusia en route, like his hero Lord Byron, to the Middle East. It was something of a pilgrimage, for his Sephardic ancestors had lived in Spain until the expulsion of the Jews, and the glowing enthusiasm of his letters home owed much to what seemed a miraculous recovery from black depressions, caused largely by financial worries, which had threatened complete nervous breakdown. He was able, he said, to spend whole days on horseback in the Serrania de Ronda, braving bandits ("if you have less than 16 dollars they shoot you"); he raved about Cadiz ("the white houses and green shutters sparkle in the sun. Figaro is in every street and Rosina in every balcony"); and "cheered at the bullfights... the sight is magnificent."

"There is a calm voluptuousness about life here that wonderfully accords with my disposition," he told his mother, adding that though he favoured rosy English blondes he thought "las Espagnolas very interesting," despite their sallow complexions and early over-plumpness ("they too soon indulge in the magnificence of en bon point"). They were at their most seductive in the twilight paseo when, in their mantillas, "with their soft dark eyes dangerously conspicuous, you willingly believe in their universal beauty... Of their hair they are very proud... All day long, even the lowest order, they are brushing, curling and arranging it."

He was much intrigued by "the language of fans" as interpreted by an *andaluza*: "Now she unfurls it with the slow pomp and conscious elegance of a peacock, now flutters it with all the languor of a listless beauty, now with all the liveliness of a vivacious one... Dolores taps you on your elbow ; you turn to listen and Florentina pokes you in the side." He himself, going native, had bought some fans ("If you think 1 have grown extraordinarily effeminate, learn that in this scorching clime the soldier will not mount guard without one"). He supplies recipes for *olla podrida* and for tomato sauce ("the Spaniards eat the Tomato in all possible ways") and recommends a two-hour siesta as "conducive to health." But above all he radiates a "Saracenic ardour... Spain is the only land for travel... Splendid buildings which make you hourly regret the expulsion of the Saracens. The Alhambra is the most imaginative, the most delicate and fantastic creation that ever sprang up on a Summer night in a fairy tale."

Disraeli's letters, when relayed through an extensive network of family and friends, may well have helped to spread the growing cult of the exotic Moorish southland and to encourage its vogue as a resort for ailing Britons. But it was Washington Irving, a far less brilliant

The Scottish artist David Wilkie urged Washington Irving to write "something with adash of the Arabian spice which pervades everything in Spain" These evocative engravings, as here of the valley of the river Darro, complemented Irving's engaging fables.

writer, who really put Andalusia on the tourist map. His *Tales of the Alhambra* sold hugely and an hotel named after him was built near the fortress-cum-palace which, he insisted, was "to the traveller imbued with a feeling for the historical and the poetical, so intertwined in the annals of romantic Spain, as much an object of devotion as is the Caaba to all true Moslems."

A born popularizer, Irving concentrates on the picturesqueness that appealed to a well-off bourgeoisie beginning to think of holidays abroad. For him "the most miserable inn is as full of adventure as an enchanted castle"; he praises "the half-wild yet frank and hospitable manners which impart such a true game-flavour to dear old romantic Spain"; and asserts that with the Spaniard "poverty is no disgrace. It sits upon him with a grandiose style, like his ragged cloak. He is an *hidalgo* even when in rags."

He was charmed by the dilapidation of the Alhambra ("bats nestling during the days in dark corners, and flitting mysteriously about the twilight chambers"); and he shrewdly sketches in a cast of lovable tatterdemalions. Mateo Ximenez, who appointed himself Irving's guide, lived in a tumbledown shack, but like other "sons of the Alhambra" who claimed that their families had been there since the final reconquest, he prided himself on his lineage ("I know we belong to some great family or other, but I forget whom") and on being "a *cristiano viejo* without any taint of Moor or Jew."

From the windows of crumbling towers hung newlywashed but threadbare clothes, "those standards of poverty." Mateo's father, a ribbon-weaver, inhabited a reed-and-plaster hut above the main gate. The only martial note was struck by the presence of some veteran soldiers, including "a brave and battered old colonel" who boasted of serving under George Washington in the American War of Independence.

In this comic-opera Eden a favourite pastime on summer evenings was "to fish, with fly-baited hooks, for the swallows which sport about the towers in myriads... With the ingenuity of arrant idlers the ragged sons of the Alhambra have thus invented the art of angling in the sky."

As a refuge from the sultry heat, Irving, who stayed in the Alhambra, used the cool, dusky crypts of what had been the baths of the Emir's harem, and at night swam in "the great reservoir of the main court." Sometimes he explored the surrounding hills with Mateo, who told him that lights flickering at nightfall along the sierra were "fires made by the men who gather snow and ice. They take turns, some to rest and warm themselves, while others fill the mules' panniers. They set off down the mountain to reach the gates of Granada before sunrise. That Sierra Nevada, Señor, is a lump of ice in the middle of Andalusia, to keep it cool in summer."

Urged by the Scottish painter David Wilkie, with whom he had visited "some of the old cities of Spain," to write "something in the Haroun Alraschid style that should have a dash of that Arabian spice which pervades everything in Spain," Irving obliged with a series of legends heard, he says, at the sundown *tertulias* presided over by Tia Antonia, the aged custodian. She and other Alhambrans were well primed with wondrous tales involving hidden Moorish gold, phantom Moorish warriors, lovesick Moslem princesses pining for handsome Spanish lovers, or greedy Spanish officials foiled in the search for treasure (usually located by deserving peasants).

Of these legends, which Irving retold with much fanciful embroidery, Théophile Gautier, one of a notable number of French romantics in Spain, remarked that "in Granada the most trifling Moorish ruin is endowed with ten or twelve miles of underground passages and a buried hoard protected by some spell or other." But even Gautier lost his sardonic cool when in 1840 he arrived in Andalusia, for him the real, or at least most flavoursome, Spain. Women with "a long, pale, oval face, great black eyes beneath velvety eyebrows, a slender, rather arched nose, a mouth as red as a pomegranate, and over all a warm golden tone." *Flamenco* dancers who "looked like women dancing, not dancing-women... They do not go in for those terrible excesses in flexibility and so escape that leanness which gives French ballets such a macabre, anatomical touch."

He even got to like garlicky gazpacho, and ordered a costume "with a pot of flowers embroidered in the middle of the back" in emulation of "lower class majos or exquisites." And he rated the four nights he spent in the Alhambra as "the most delicious moments in my life. We had set up our headquarters in the Court of the Lions; and our furniture consisted of two mattresses, a copper lamp, an earthenware jar, and a few bottles of sherry which we set to cool in the fountain." Certainly the place had been neglected, but the worst menace to the charms of the Alhambra and the Generalife was whitewash, "renewed with a desperately persistent cleanliness... The brush of the whitewasher has caused the disappearance of more masterpieces than the scythe of Time." Even so the Alhambra was infinitely preferable to the oppressive, if majestic, gloom of the Escorial, which Gautier considered "an architectural nightmare... a gigantic polypus of granite."

Granada, gushed Dumas, was "like a sleepy maid resting in the sunshine". But he was disenchanted by gypsy musicians and dancers - "with grubby, gaudy dresses and big, grimy feet... We had asked for real gypsies; now we had them."

The very thought of the Escorial made Gautier shudder, and in Granada too he had moments of despair. No doubt it was unreasonable to expect its bourgeois citizens "to go about, for the greater glory of local colour, in the burnous of Boabdil's time or the iron armour of the time of Ferdinand and Isabella." But must they be so grimly anti-picturesque, so determined to prove their modernity by wearing drably formal French clothes? "When one praises the wild beauty of their land," he lamented, "they apologize for having as yet no railways, no factories driven by steam, no gas for the street lamps." Alas "a most disheartening uniformity" was "pervading the world under some vague pretext of progress...

What use to make a long journey at speed only to see more Rues de la Paix lighted by gas and filled with comfortable bourgeois?"

In Madrid Gautier had found *cerveza con limón* and *horchata de chufa* excellent thirst quenchers (with typical perversity here commended visiting countries "at their extreme season. Spain in summer. Russia in winter"). He liked the cries of the street vendors, Galician water-carriers and ever-present "lightermen," "for what Madrid needs most after water is a light for its cigarettes; and so the cry of *fuego, fuego* mingles constantly with that of *agua, agua.* This fire is borne by young rascals in little bowls full of charcoal and fine ashes, with a handle to prevent one from burning one's fingers."

Along the Prado he was gratified to see few women's hats and plenty of lace mantillas. For "in a mantilla a woman must be as ugly as the seven cardinal virtues not to look pretty." But again alas, "the lower folds of the mantilla float over an odious shawl, and this is accompanied by some ordinary dress which in no way recalls the full Spanish petticoat."

Though contemptuous of bourgeois humanitarianism, he was startled to hear loungers in the Puerta del Sol casually discussing Carlist atrocities of a kind "that have come to be thought bad form by the Cherokees." But then, he was told, these events had taken place in Old Castile and so were of merely abstract interest.

"This," says Gautier, "gives the key to many things which seem incomprehensible when viewed from France... To the inhabitants of New Castile what happens in Old Castile is as irrelevant as what goes on in the moon. From the political standpoint Spain does not yet exist... it still consists of peoples speaking different dialects and unable to bear each other."

There seemed to be plenty of weapons available for settling scores. He admired the "fancy cutlery" on sale at Albacete, wicked-looking knives whose blades bore such mottoes as *cuando ésta vívara pica, no hay remedio en la botica* (for this viper's sting, no remedy at the chemist). It was even said that "adepts can recognize the artist responsible for a wound from the look of it."

The danger from brigands, however, had in his experience been much exaggerated ("we never saw anything to justify panic. Nevertheless a little fear keeps you alert and saves you from boredom"). But Gautier's studied flippancy fades, to be replaced by the solemn intensity of an instant—and highly articulate—intellectual convert when he writes about corridas. Furiously he denies that bullfights are uncivilized, passionately argues that the drama of the moment of truth, the kill, is "worth all the plays of Shakespeare," He revels in a marathon of slaughter in Málaga: "The same combatants held the ring for three days, during which 24 bulls were killed and 96 horses left dead upon the sand."

Like Joseph Baretti, Gautier reckoned that the art of idling, so perfected in Andalusia, had been polished by necessity. With so little work to be had, many young men settled for a life of decorative inactivity. This could have an almost aristocratic appeal: "none of that frenzied restlessness which vexes the people of the North... Work in general is, in the eyes of these Spaniards, a humiliating thing unworthy of a free man."

When at the end of his tour Gautier, the monocled, bourgeois-baiting inventor of the art-for-art's-sake creed, arrived in Gibraltar, the culture shock was unnerving ("from Moorish cities you suddenly drop into Ramsgate"). A final trauma was the sight of an Englishwoman "wearing a hat with a green veil and striding like a grenadier with her large feet shod in large boots" (so unlike the tiny, satin-slippered feet of his adored *sevillanas*). "I felt quite ashamed," he writes, "of the extravagant embroideries of my sky-blue cloak. For the first time in six months I became aware that I was not properly dressed and did not look like a gentleman."

In October 1846 Alexandre Dumas, beside whom Gautier was a cult writer with a limited readership, made a triumphal Spanish progress. Then at the height of his international fame as novelist and playwright, his first travel book, *In Switzerland*, had greatly increased French tourism there, and it was hoped that he could do the same for Spain. He probably did, for his commentary is well garnished with

During his stay in the Alhambra, Washington Irving listened to wondrous tales told in the evening, (sometimes as here, in the Court of the Myrtles), by the custodian, "the good old maiden dame," Tia Antonia.

picturesque come-hitherisms—the literary equivalents of Gustave Doré's etchings. Spain, says Dumas, is his "longed-for country of Romance." Madrid is full of "women lovely beneath their rags, proud men dignified in tattered clothing... those velvet eyes that lured Byron from English beauties; those dainty hands that flutter the quick, shrill fan; those tiny feet that could wear Cinderella's slipper." Andalusia is "a gay, lovely land with castanets in her hands and a garland on her brow." At a bullfight he is "so strongly moved" that he feels "none of the revulsion I had been promised. I, who cannot bear to see the cook kill a chicken, could not tear my eyes away from the bull that had already slain three horses and sorely wounded a human being."

Travelling with an entourage—his son (recovering from a tragic love affair later written up as *La Dame aux Camélias*), his Arab valet, his chief literary collaborator, and three French artists—Dumas was treated *en prince*. The queen made him a Knight Commander of the Order of Charles III. Customs officers did not detain the author of *The Count of Monte Cristo*. In Seville he was asked to choose the pro-gramme at the principal theatre for as long as he stayed in town. Heavily armed against bandits (I publicly announced that we "shall rob *them*"), Dumas's party had no trouble that way, but did not, according to him, hesitate to threaten recalcitrant innkeepers, especially when they proposed to give English guests preferential treatment.

A recurrent complaint is of the roads: "even if the coach does not capsize, it bounces high in the air at least twice before it can settle on all four wheels again... May Heaven grant me, in my old age, the boon of becoming a Spanish roadmender, whose great mission in life is to swathe himself in his cloak and watch travellers suffer."

But Dumas liked the colourfulness of "the triple stage-coach team of *mayoral, sotocochero* and *zagal*, with their picturesque uniform of pointed hats, velvet-trimmed jackets, red belts, wide-cut breeches, and top boots or sandals"; appreciated "the endless variety of costumes in the different regions which have grudgingly consented to form one kingdom, but will never bind themselves into a united people"; and lyrically described the saffron fields around Manzanares—"a delightful little town... No end to the sound of singing and the throbbing of guitars. The lower room in every house is crowded with young girls removing the pistils from saffron flowers. Heaps of purplish petals reach to the ceiling, emphasising the fresh complexion and velvety eyes of the toilers."

Granada, gushed Dumas, was "like a sleepy maiden resting in the sunshine on a bed of moss and bracken, ringed round with cactus plants and aloes." As for the Generalife, "nowhere in the world will you find in such a small expanse such fragrance, such freshness, such a multitude of windows, each opening on a corner of paradise." But the spell was broken when, at a command *flamenco* performance, the "illustrious foreigners" showed their distaste for the "dirtiness and depravity" of the gypsy artistes. As "a man of the world" Dumas could have tolerated the erotic implications. But not, it seems, from teenage girls "with matted, unkempt hair," swarthy faces, grubby, gaudy dresses and big, grimy feet. He had expected "dancers with delicate hands, dainty feet, and a skin of white or gold." But after all "we had asked for real gypsies: now we had them." (Sanitized "savages" for civilized tourists was the message.)

In Seville, like Gautier (from whose travelogue he borrows freely), Dumas bought some *majo* finery, and "a whole set of mule-harness, pompoms, little bells and all (I hope to startle Longchamps with it!)." He also visited "the huge tobacco factory which makes three-quarters of Europe's cigars. It is amazing to see its 1,300 pretty young work-girls all smoking in the street like veterans or chewing tobacco like old sailors... They are allowed to use as much tobacco as they like in working hours, and if some also finds its way into their pockets that may explain why no *cigarrera* is ever without her escort of a young sub-altern or a handsome officer of the merchant navy."

It was a *cigarrera* who, in Prosper Mérimée's novella Carmen and in Bizet's opera based upon it, typified the *gitanesca* Spain of the romantic imagination. Moody and fickle, factory girl turned bandits' moll and decoy, *flamenco* dancer and *torero*-fancier, Carmen focused all the pungent ingredients in one flamboyant and finally tragic figure. Mérimée described his spellcasting gypsy in terms well calculated to attract readers tired of the genteel heroines of conventional fiction. Hers is "a strange but savage beauty... the eyes, slanting but admirably shaped, had an expression at once sensual and wild," an expression accentuated by her flirting of the folds of a black mantilla. Carmen's lips, "a little thick, allowed one to see teeth whiter than peeled almonds. Her hair, possibly a little coarse, was black, with glints of blue like a crow's wing." And she was maddeningly independent—a promiscuous, untameable creature.

Mérimée was one of the many lovers of George Sand (Baroness Aurore de Dudevant, née Dupin), who as novelist and free spirit—a kind of sophisticated Carmen figure—had become the uncrowned Queen of Romantics. As such, and expecting due recognition of her celebrity, she arrived in Majorca in November 1838 with her two young children, Maurice and Solange, and her current lover, the Polish musician-composer Frédéric Chopin. Her motives were mixed. A warmer climate, she thought, might be good for the sickly Maurice and for the tuberculous Chopin. She wanted to have Chopin to herself, away from the gossip of Paris; she had vague dreams of an Arcadian idyll among "noble savage" peasants; and she hoped to find fresh inspiration to finish a novel.

The real Majorca gave a jolt to her sensibilities and preconceptions beside which Dumas's disgust with real gypsies was a mere trifle.

For a start, hardly anyone seemed to know who she was. Palma was crammed with refugees from the Carlist war on the mainland, accommodation was hard to find and basic if not squalid when found. Chopin's precious piano was impounded by the customs. His health deteriorated in the heavy rain and snow of an exceptionally inclement winter—severest in the former Carthusian monastery, high in the mists of Valldemosa, where from December George Sand and her family spent two trying months before returning to France.

Nothing, she wrote soon afterwards, could have been more gothically romantic than the monastery, peopled with former monks and a scattering of eccentrics weirder and more sinister than those in Irving's Alhambra. The "more than Alpine" prospects were superb.

But the mountain tracks were often impassable. Hostile peasants threw stones at the "evil" strangers who never went to church and allowed Solange to roam about alone in a jacket and trousers "like a man." Such society as she found in Palma among the local nobility was so densely ignorant as to seem "more African than European". Priests anathematized this Gallic Jezebel and she ridiculed them (suggesting that the lecherous monks of Valldemosa had fathered most of the villagers) and sneered at "imbecilic" hermits who exploited "feudal" superstition. The peasants, "thieving yet innocent," were little better than chimpanzees. She nicknamed Majorca "Monkey Island" and despaired of raising such Calibans from the mud in which, like their beloved pigs, they actually liked to wallow.

Through it all the ailing Chopin managed to comlete his *Preludes*, romantic masterpieces "full of the scent of paradise." But when Sand's literary revenge, *A Winter in Majorca*, was published she was denounced in the *Diario de Palma* as "the most immoral of writers and the most obscene of women." Chopin, though he too had shown aristocratic disdain for local bumpkins, was pitied as the victim of a nymphomaniac harpy. But all this was forgotten when, a century or so later, the Valldemosan interlude, of which George Sand wrote that "too high a price can be paid for one or two transports of admiration and one or two hours of romantic ecstasy wrested from ill fortune," played its sanitized part in radically changing the Majorcan way of life. A period of considerable strain, during which she tried to keep her children happy, worried about Chopin, and nursed him with devotion, was to be lucratively mythologized as a honeymoon of genius so uninterruptly rhapsodic as to justify the touristic slogan "Majorca, Isle of Love."

V

BIBLES ON SPAIN

Richard Ford and George Borrow

In 1833 Richard Ford, a gentleman of independent means who had previously travelled widely on the continent and had gained a reputation as a discerning art collector, returned to England from Spain with dozens of bulging notebooks and more than 500 sketches. Few Spanish artists had bothered to memorialize their native scene, so that the drawings and watercolours done by Ford and by his wife Harriet are often the only record of buildings and localities which have vanished or changed beyond recognition. That in itself was a remarkable achievement; and the notebooks were the raw material for a magnum opus that, mingling romantic zest and pungent, often splenetic realism, remains the classic coverage of Spain by a foreigner.

Omniscient yet unpedantic, plundering earlier writers but personalizing a mass of information, the bulky *Handbook for Travellers in Spain* (1845), whose format is followed by the present Blue Guide, and the handier, more popular *Gatherings from Spain* (1846), set new standards in their genre.

Ford's outspoken prejudices, typical of a High Tory grandee of the time, make him the more readable. Unencumbered by false modesty or careful impartiality, he is as stoutly anti-papist and Francophobic as his friend George Borrow. Notwithstanding industrial strife and political agitation, Britannia ruled the waves, her upper class was superbly self-confident, and Ford did not hide his conviction that, in the words of the historian Lord Macaulay, he belonged to "the most enlightened generation of the most enlightened people that ever existed."

So caustic were some passages in the *Handbook*—one of a pioneering series of detailed guides published by John Murray, whose house at Wimbledon was nicknamed "Handbook Hall"—that the 1844 edition was suppressed, costing Ford much money and some intensive cutting and rewriting. The final version which, with the help of a Spanish correspondent, Don Pascual de Gayangos, had taken five years to complete, was still bristlingly opinionated for, as Ford told Murray, "I can't cool my style to the tune of a way-bill... the words come boiling over like a sodawater bottle."

With more than 1,000 closely-printed pages of text, 140 itineraries and a 50-page index, it was quite expensive. But its "rich and rare" (Ford's words) combination of "learning and facetiousness" boosted sales, as no doubt did his influential friends and acquaintances, among them the Duke of Wellington.

Gatherings, designed primarily for "the ladies," was a runaway success.

During his long "labour of love" Ford kept in constant touch with Murray, tartly commenting on rivals who beat him into print or whose works he consulted for revised editions of the Handbook. Even Borrow comes in for criticism ("El Gitano has taken my advice in good part... but here and there has got swampt in that damnable slough—fine writing"). Inglis, who needing money had rushed out his valuable reportage in a matter of months, is dismissed as "long addled by over-bookmaking." Ticknor gets some faint praise, but Gautier is put down as "very French, clever and superficial, of no earthly use except to amuse the Parisians, who are more ignorant than the Cockneys of London."

Ford himself had followed Jardine's recipe for serious travel: a base (in fact two, Seville in winter, Granada in summer), several extensive tours, affection for his own country, and female company (Harriet

Richard Ford, gentleman traveller and author of the massive, quirky *Handbook for Travellers in Spain*, poses in *majo* (dandy) costume during his Spanish period.

Ford accompanied him on some trips). Yet when in the autumn of 1830 the Fords, with three young children and three female domestics, rented a house in the Plazuela San Isidro in Seville, there was little thought of a prolonged stay, let alone of writing a handbook (it was Murray who suggested that in 1839). Harriet, who was pregnant, had been advised to winter in a warmer climate. Meaning to make the most, socially speaking, of this interlude, she and Richard had begun to study Spanish grammar on the voyage to Gibraltar. Three years later Ford had criss-crossed Spain from end to end, mostly on horseback with an Andalusian attendant.

He collected more than 150 passport entries and, as a precaution, purchased a safe-conduct from the Andalusian bandit boss José Maria, El Tempranillo. In Ford's opinion passports were "the curse of continental travel to which a free-born Briton never can get reconciled," and he chafed at the self-importance of petty officials who could be "as deaf alike to the dictates of common sense or humanity as adders or Berbers." At Elche he was nearly arrested for sketching the palm groves and in Castile was taken into custody for the offence of drawing a Roman ruin. Almost as unnerving was the curiosity of staring natives who clearly thought him eccentric if not insane.

Perhaps such incidents were responsible for the more churlish judgements in the *Handbook*, since as Rose Macaulay commented, "the insults expurgated from the first edition can scarcely be worse than those left in it." Catalonia, he writes, "is no place for the man of pleasure, taste or literature... here cotton is spun, vice and discontent bred, revolution concocted." Valencians are characterized as "vindictive, sullen, fickle and treacherous." In Murcia "the better classes vegetate in a monotonous unsocial existence; their pursuits are the cigar and the siesta... The lower classes are superstitious, litigious and revengeful." Jerez is "a straggling, ill-kept Moorish city," and as for Málaga "one day will suffice. It has few attractions beyond climate, almonds and raisins and sweet wine."

Madrid he considered "a second-rate, inhospitable city" and most provincial towns had "a convent-like, dead look... even an artist, when he has finished his sketches, is ready to commit suicide from sheer Bore, the genius of the locality." Extremaduran villages were so obsessed with pig-raising that they could "more correctly be termed coalitions of pigsties." And the passion for pork which had so disgusted George Sand might be explained as a defiance of "the pork-eschewing Jew or Moor"; so that "the eating or not eating the flesh of an animal deemed unclean by the impure infidel became a test of orthodoxy... and good bacon is wedded to sound doctrine."

Even the Alhambra, "the pearl and magnet of Granada," was for many Spaniards "little better than a *casa de ratones*, a rat's hole, which in truth they have endeavoured to make it by centuries of neglect... They resent almost as heretical the preference shown by foreigners to the works of infidels rather than to those of good Catholics." Ford employed a squad of carpenters and painters to smarten up a suite of rooms once occupied by the governor and recently vacated by the Tia Antonia of Washington Irving's Tales. But he could do nothing

The crumbling prison of the Inquisition in Cordoba. Borrow, who made three missionary tours 1836-40, found Cordoba "a mean, dark, gloomy place", but relished tales of heresy and witchcraft told by an aged priest once employed by the Inquisition.

about the noise of rattling chains which filled the air as galley-slaves laboured to convert part of the palace into a storehouse for salt fish.

Despite his remarks about Extremaduran villages, Ford found the hams of Montanchez so delicious that he introduced them (together with amontillado sherry) into England. And despite its melancholy decay, and the death of his baby son from injuries received in a fall from a crumbling staircase, the Alhambra inspired one of the *Handbook*'s most eloquent passages. Too much sentimental nonsense, he said with his customary air of superior disdain, had been written about a place which, to be truly appreciated, had to be "lived in and beheld in the semi-obscure evening, so beautiful of itself in the South... All is again given up to the past... The wan rays of the moon tip the filigree arches and give a misty, undefined magnitude to the saloons beyond." Sounds from the city below, baying dogs or a tinkling guitar, served to "increase the Alhambra's desolation. Then do the fancy and the imagination come alive... The shadows of the cypresses on the walls assume the forms of the dusky Moor revisiting his last home, while the night winds, breathing through the unglazed windows and the myrtles, rustle as his silken robes or sigh like his lament over the profanation of the unclean infidel and destroyer."

Life in Seville was marred by "the defects of Spanish servants... procrastination, waste, improvidence and untidiness"; and knocking a fine but comfortless mansion into satisfactory shape (more alterations) was a tiresome business.

But one did not have to stray far beyond the confines of polite society to put such minor nuisances into perspective. "Often," writes Ford in one of his dramatic set-pieces, "have we seen the frightful deathtray standing upright at the doors of the humble, with a human outline marked on the wood by the deathdamp of a hundred previous burdens... Such bodies are cast into the trenches like those of dogs, often naked, as the survivors or sextons strip them even of their rags. Those poorer still, who cannot afford the trifling fees, sometimes, during the night, suspend the corpses of their children in baskets near the cemetery porch. I once beheld a cloaked Spaniard pacing mournfully in the burial ground of Seville. When the public trench was opened he drew from beneath the folds the dead body of his child, cast it in, and disappeared. Thus half the world lives without knowing how the other half dies."

Doctoring was derisive. Ferdinand VII had been persuaded to close medical schools as nests of heresy, innovation and potential revolution, opening instead "a tauromachian university. Men indeed might be mangled, but bulls were to be mercifully put out of their misery with the honours of science." Quack remedies abounded, often to the profit of the Church, as at Ignatius Loyola's cave-shrine at Manresa, where "pulverized stones," allegedly from the sanctified rock, were sold and swallowed by the faithful.

Was it to be wondered at that, in a land of such brutal poverty, weighed down with taxes on imported goods, smugglers and bandits were admired? The real brigands, says Ford, were to be encountered "not on the road but in confessional boxes, lawyers' offices, and still more in the bureaux of government." What were the 5,000 Civil Guards, modelled on the French gendarmerie, who by the 1840s had been set to patrol the country, but "rogues employed to keep down the expression of indignant public opinion and, instead of catching thieves, in upholding those first-rate criminals, foreign and domestic, who are now robbing poor Spain of her gold and liberties?" Bandits being pathetically superstitious, the Church took its cut of ill-gotten gains. "Mountain confessors of the Friar Tuck order, animated by a pious love for dollars when expended in expiatory masses, consider the payment such a laudable restitution as to entitle the contrite culprit to ample absolution."

The smuggler (mostly of tobacco, in defiance of a royal monopoly) was "the hero of the Spanish stage, and comes on equipped in full costume, with his blunderbuss, to sing the well-known *Yo que soy contrabandista ¡Yo ho!* to the delight of all listeners from the Straits of Gibraltar to the Bidassoa, well-bribed custom-house officers not excepted."

18th-century travellers had noted a passion for smoking, and Ford explains that "it levels all ranks and proves that democracy under a despotism which exists in smoking Spain as in the torrid East." The cigar or the cigarette (a Spanish invention) was, he suggests, "the habeas corpus of Spanish liberties. The soldier takes fire from the canon's lip, and the dark face of the humble labourer is whitened by the reflection from the cigar of the grandee."

To smoke was to defy Authority. Without a cigar or cigarette in his mouth a Spaniard would "resemble a house without a chimney, a steamer without a funnel." It might be argued that too much time and money was wasted in the serious business of smoking and that the importing of tobacco was "even a more doubtful good than that of potatoes to cognate Ireland, where it fosters poverty and population." But it was surely understandable that a Spaniard should "steep in sweet oblivious stupefaction the misery of being fretted by empty larders,

A *corrida de toros* with *picador* in action. Ford, noting that bullfights were blessed by the Church, saw the corrida as a substitute for the Inquisition's *autos de fe*, with the bull playing the role of condemned heretic for the delight of the masses.

vicious political institutions, and a very hot climate." It would probably be more politic to encourage than to penalize the habit, since it was widely believed that "it deadens the Spaniards' overexcitable imagination and appeases their too exquisite nervous sensibility."

Fatal stabbings and "a general indifference to life which almost amounts to oriental fatalism" were, he thought, caused partly from life among the many being at best a struggle for existence. "When one is removed there is somewhat less difficulty for the survivors; hence everyone is for himself and for today. *El último mono se ahoga*, the last monkey is drowned, or as we say, the devil take the hindmost."

The Inquisition, finally abolished in 1820, had been a popular institution, a leveller more likely to strike at the rich than at the insignificant poor. Now the bullfight was not only, as Ticknor had divined, a symbol of unrepentant *hispanidad* but a useful focus for violent emotions which might otherwise explode in riot or rebellion. Ford saw the corrida as a substitute for the *auto de fe*, with the bull playing the role of condemned heretic (the clergy, "enemies of the theatre," were "friends of the amphitheatre"). Used to drunken, brawling English mobs, particularly at election time, he enjoyed the tumult of the crowd ("now his majesty the many reigns triumphant"); and while maintaining that a massive British bull would give the *toreros* some serious opposition, he denied that the bloody spectacle was harmful to morals (where was family life so affectionate as in Spain?) Its real fault lay in its sheer repetitious monotony.

Yet a *gran corrida* was a sight not be missed, as "the brilliant army of combatants separate like a bursting shell and take up their respective places as regularly as our fielders at a cricket match." For Spaniards it was also, "church excepted, the only public meeting allowed... the tip-top aesthetic treat, as the Italian Opera is in England," but one "shared by high and low, vulgar and exquisite alike." Ford reasons that "moments of painful detail are lost in the poetical ferocity of the whole, for the interest of the tragedy of real death is irresistible and all-absorbing... the plaza is the focus of a fire which blood alone can extinguish." A fighting bull did not, after all, have such a bad life. "He roams in ample pastures through a youth and manhood free from toil, and when killed in the plaza only anticipates by a few months the certain fate of the over-laboured, mutilated ox." Finally, it was well to remember that "the bull is always put at once out of his misery and never exposed to the lingering death of the poor wounded hare... We must not see a *toro* in Spanish eyes and wink at the fox in our own, nor "compound for vices we're inclined to/By damning those we have no mind to."

Outside the bullring, about which he wrote with such vivid authority, Ford was happiest on the road, riding over tracks with "ruts deep as ancient prejudices." He disliked coach travel, "for a man in a public carriage ceases to be an individual." Leaving behind the elegant *majo* costume he sometimes wore in Seville and Granada, he dressed in the expeditionary gear which he recommended to adventurous readers: a jacket of black sheepskin or lambskin, "a sash round the waist which sustains the loins and maintains an equable heat over the abdomen," and a cloak or *manta* (striped plaid). In summer "the head should be protected with a silk handkerchief tied after a turban fashion, which all the natives do, in addition we always lined the inside of our hats with thickly-doubled brown paper." To combat the dust and glare of steppes where scarce rain "dries up quicker than a woman's tears," he advocates "a pair of blue gauze wire goggles... The best remedy is to bathe the eyes frequently with hot water and never to rub them when inflamed, except with the elbows, *los ojos con los codos.*"

Aware that bad government and wretched communications were the root cause of poverty and sloth, Ford also knew that they had perpetuated the picturesque survivals which so powerfully attracted him. He relished the rough, jostling vitality of byway hostelries, the pungent varieties of local pride, the baroque maxims that glorified the imperial past or justified national failings: "If God were not God he would be king of the Spains." Or the reply of the Blessed Virgin when petitioned to give good government to her darling realm: "That can never be granted, for if it were, not an angel would remain a day longer in heaven."

Spaniards, he noted, seldom travelled for pleasure. "Why indeed should they, since each man's own parish is the central spot of Spain's glory." Many inns therefore retained "much the same state of primitive dirt and discomfort which most of those on the Continent presented until repolished by our hints and guineas... The racy Peninsula is too little travelled for its natives to adopt the increasing conveniences of the Swiss, that nation of innkeepers and coach-jobbers."

In the 1830s a parador was still "a huge caravansery for the reception of waggons, carts and beasts of burden." To get any attention a traveller had to bribe his host—*más habla el dinero que palabras de caballero*—and, just as important, "the coolness of a determined Englishman's manner, when in earnest, is what few foreigners can withstand."

With some *posaderos*, however, complaint was useless. "If you tell the landlord that his wine is more sour than his vinegar, he will

Gustave Doré's dramatic etching of beggars outside Burgos cathedral. Such picturesque squalor was an essential ingredient of Irving's "dear old romantic Spain ... poverty is no disgrace. It sits upon a Spaniard with a grandiose style, like his ragged cloak. He is an hidalgo even in rags."

gravely reply, "Señor, that cannot be, for both came out of the same cask!" Useless, too, to expect comfort in ventas where chairs were unknown and people sat on the ground "as in the East, or on low stools, and fall to in a most Oriental manner with an un-European ignorance of forks; for which they substitute a short wooden or horn spoon or dip their bread in the dish, or fish up morsels with their long pointed knives. They eat copiously but with gravity... for none of any nation, as a mass, are better bred or mannered than the lower classes of Spaniards."

Such oriental customs extended to the justly renowned mule-teer. "His generic term is *arriero*, a geeupper, for his *arre, arre* is pure Arabic, as indeed are almost all the terms connected with his craft, since the Moriscos were long the great carriers of Spain." Mules and donkeys, as stubborn as their drivers, were untenderly treated. Terms of endearment might be tried, but they were likely to be followed by kicks and blows, something which was commonly accepted, "just as a philanthropic Yankee has a right to wallop his own nigger."

Ford's conservative, or conservationist, instincts rebelled at the thought of railways invading the landscape, bringing "progressive" notions of "comfortable scurry." Surely the muleteers of Spain would fiercely resist such a deplorable innovation, even to the point of sabotage? Surely they would "never permit the bread to be taken out of their mouths by this Lutheran locomotive?" Writing to Murray, Ford predicted that the necessary capital would not be raised, that "the thing will not be carried out," and that the British engineers "sent to bare and gouge the sierras" would be thwarted by natural barriers and ignominiously recalled.

He enjoyed basic Spanish food, *ollas* and *pucheros*, and even reconciled himself to *garbanzos*, "the potato of Spain." It pleased him that in "the genuine Spanish interior" wayfaring was "calculated for the *pack*, as in England a century ago... The inns, roads and right sides suit the natives and their brutes." Nor was it likely that "in a land which hovers between Europe and Africa, between the hat and the turban," the system would be modified "to please the fancies of a stranger." Spain, in fact, was "a land bottled up for the antiquarian" where folk cultures had not yet been obliterated by the pressures of an industrial revolution. In *Gatherings* Ford praises flamenco dancing ("no cruel stays fetter the serpentine flexibility, the impassioned abandon of the daughters of the South"); and in a vigorous peroration he lambasts the "Manchester missionaries" who preach unrelenting 14-hour-day toil to their "immelodious and unsaltatory operatives." Such denatured robots did not know what to do with themselves, beyond getting drunk or deadening their misery with opium, when idle, whereas to most Spaniards idleness was "a foretaste of the bliss of heaven, while occupation, thought in England to be happiness, is the treadmill doom of the lost forever."

But the Manchester gospel was gaining ground, the threat of "progress," as represented by mincing French "civilization," loomed. Embarrassed by picturesque decay, educated Spaniards thought this distinguished visitor was making fun of them when he enthused over aspects of their country which were "Roman, African, or in a word,

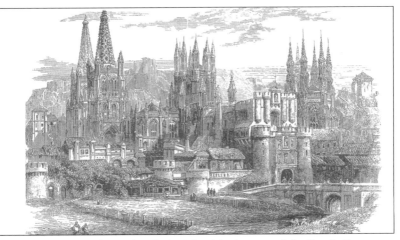

For tourists not obsessed with the Moorish glamour of the South, Burgos, with its mighty Gothic cathedral and its associations with the legendary Cid, became a romantic mecca in northern Spain.

un-European." Toledo and Cuenca, to them, were "ugly, odious old cities, because the tortuous, narrow lanes do not run in rows as straight as Pall Mall or the Rue de Rivoli. How depressing that such well-meaning reformers should envisage the ideal city as a place of rectangular uniformity "paved with broad flags and lighted with gas, in which Spaniards can walk about dressed as Englishmen and Spanish women like those of France."

"Mantillas are going, alas! The relentless march of European intellect is crushing many a native wild flower." Yet change was inevitable. Analysing tourist reactions to a corrida, Ford remarked that most Spaniards "scarcely notice the cruel incidents which engross and horrify the foreigner, who on his part is equally blind to those redeeming excellencies on which alone the attention of the rest of the spectators is fixed; the tables are turned against the stranger, whose aesthetic mind's eye can see the poetry and beauty of the picturesque rags and tumbledown hamlets... and yet is blinded to the poverty, misery

An Andalusian landscape which sometimes, said Irving, "partook of the stern and solitary character of Africa" and which reminded Ford that Spain was "a land which hovers between Europe and Africa, between the hat and the turban."

and want of civilization to which alone the vision of the higher-classed native is directed."

Ford, "as frisky as a five-year-old" at the success of his two volumes, had warmly commended *The Bible in Spain* to Murray ("Borrow is such a *trump*, as full of meat as an egg, and a fresh-laid one at that"). It would sell, he promised, and he was right.

George Borrow's *fantasia* or *picaresque* romance, which reveals less about Spain than about his own tormented ego, made him for a while as famous as Dickens or Thackeray. It remains a classic—of creative autobiography, the work of a paranoiac who lived intensely in a world of his own imagining. A selftaught linguist, he had been plucked from a life of vagabond obscurity by the British and Foreign Bible Society, for which he had already worked in Russia. Only at the last moment did he abandon his ambition to travel to China, deciding instead to honour Spain with his presence.

At 32 he was in full vigour, with a special interest in gypsies, whose language and customs he had mastered to the extent of being accepted as an honorary Romany. And he did not hesitate to use the Society's funds to gather off-beat material. He had been instructed to arrange for the printing in Madrid, and distribution in central Spain, of 5,000 copies of the new Testament in Castilian. But he spent much time in remote parts of Galicia (where, he says, he was mistaken for the pretender Don Carlos) and in Extremadura and Andalusia among the gypsies, for whom he decided to produce a St Luke's gospel in their own tongue. He was already at work on a St Luke's gospel in Basque.

Alarmed by his waywardness, the Society tried to recall him. They were not alone in their misgivings. Mendizabal, the (Jewish) liberal prime minister, thought Borrow's mission grotesquely inopportune at a time when Carlist rebels were advancing on Madrid and the need was for military aid, not Bible portions. The British ambassador, forced to extricate him from gaol, was exasperated by the self-importance of "Don Jorgito the English heretic," who extracted some lively copy from his brief and (thanks to the ambassador) comparatively comfortable imprisonment. A connoisseur of low life, he reported some bizarre encounters which seemed to uphold his contention that "Spain is the land of extraordinary characters." These included "bloods of the robber foppery" strutting about in "snow-white linen and a waistcoat of blue or green silk with an abundance of silver buttons," a housebreaker who "had committed a rather atrocious murder," and this man's seven-year-old son/accomplice. "The imp too wore the robber finery, the robber kerchief round his brow and a long Manchegan knife in the crimson *faja*." The father, he remarked, "took all imaginable care of this chick of the gallows, would dandle him on his knee and occasionally take the cigar from his own lips to insert it in the urchin's mouth."

The opening of the Despacho de la Sociedad Biblica, in the Calle del Principe near the Plaza de Cervantes, had been well publicized. Borrow had designed "three thousand posters of yellow, blue and crimson" which were pasted on walls or paraded by sandwichmen. "Pope of Rome! Look to thyself! It appears to me that the days of your sway are numbered in Spain," Don Jorge pictures himself as exulting by the window piled high with New Testaments. His life was threatened, he says: "One of the ruffians called Manolos came up to me one night in a dark street and told me that unless I discontinued selling my Jewish books I should have a knife *nailed in my heart.*" Priests circulated a rumour that he was "a sorcerer, the companion of gypsies and witches," an accusation to which he claims to have loftily replied, "That I was an associate of gypsies I do not deny. Why should I be ashamed of their company when my Master mingled with thieves and publicans?"

On the first of three missionary tours made between 1836 and 1840 Borrow had crossed from Portugal into Extremadura on "a sorry mule covered with sores, walleyed, and with a kind of halt in its gait." Tall and bearded, wearing a battered Cordoban hat and weather-beaten black cloak, he soon got acquainted with some gypsies around Badajoz: "wild Paco, the man with a withered arm who wielded the shears with his left hand; and his wife Antonia, skilled in hokkano, or the great trick. Here I first preached the gospel to the gypsy people."

Seeing washerwomen at work by the river Guadiana, he drew "some analogy between their employment and my own. I was about to tan my northern complexion by exposing myself to the hot sun of Spain in the humble hope of being able to cleanse some of the foul stains of Popery from the minds of its children, whilst they were bronzing themselves on the banks of the river in order to make white the garments of strangers." (Borrow used this analogy so often in his wayside sermons that he was sometimes assumed to be a soap-vendor.)

Reaching Cordoba soon after a rebel raid, he thought it, "a mean, dark, gloomy place without buildings worthy of attention" except for the monstrously cathedralized mosque. But though evidently preferring the Moslem religion to what he considered the idolatrous pseudo-Christianity of Rome, he enjoyed a long conversation with an aged priest who, when the Carlist guerrillas entered his village, "had gone to meet them, dressed in full canonicals, and proclaimed Carlos Quinto in the market-place." Once an official of the Inquisition, the old man discussed sexual lapses among the clergy

The Roman bridge at Cordoba. Borrow admitted that "the city's situation is beautiful" and reported an innkeeper's suggestion that "the heiress of England" should marry the son of the Pretender Don Carlos, thus encouraging more rich English visitors.

("upon the whole," Borrow reports him as saying, "we were rather tolerant, knowing the infirmities of human nature"); spoke of the menace of "black" and "white" Judaism, the latter including "all kinds of heresy, such as "Lutheranism, freemasonry and the like"; and touched upon sorcery, for instance the remarkable case of "a nun who was in the habit of flying about the convent garden over the tops of the orange trees."

"Riding on because of the word of righteousness," Borrow had some success with his Testaments in villages around Toledo. "It was well," he brags, "that heat agrees with my constitution, since the very *arrieros* frequently drop dead from their mules, smitten by sun-stroke." Sometimes, he says, "the poor labourers, being eager to obtain the scriptures and having no money, brought rabbits, fruit and barley as equivalents." Touched by their eagerness, he insists that "the genuine Spaniard" must be sought "not in seaports or large towns, but in lone villages." There the earnest traveller would find "that gravity of deportment and chivalry of disposition which Cervantes is said to have sneered away."

He had a poor opinion of Andalusians, who were ridiculed by most Spaniards "from their tendency to boasting and the incorrect manner in which they pronounce Castilian." Never at ease in formal society, he thought "the higher classes probably the most vain and foolish of human beings, with a taste for nothing but sensual amusements, foppery in dress, and ribald discourse." Yet he lavishes his most lyrical prose upon Seville, openly envying the unworthy rich "in whose Moorish patios are to be found shrubs, orange trees, and all kinds of flowers, and perhaps a small aviary, so that no situation can be conceived more delicious than to be here in the shade hearkening to the song of the birds and the voice of the fountain... Oft have I sighed that my fate did not permit me to reside in such an Eden for the remainder of my days."

He loved Seville as a setting for his version of the dashing *caballero*, rather as Hemingway was to use Spain as a stage for *macho* posturing. How pleasant in springtime "to stroll along the shores of the Guadalquivir in a grove called Las Delicias... There wander the black-eyed Andalusian damsels clad in their graceful silk mantillas; and there gallops the Andalusian cavalier on his long-tailed, thick-maned steed."

Borrow himself would career through "the long shady walks" on his splendid Arab horse, Sidi Habismilk. "His thundering hoofs were soon heard beneath the vaulted archway of the Puerto de Jerez, and in another moment he would stand stone still before the door of my solitary house in the little silent square of the Pilar Seca."

Borrow's Spanish adventure ended when the Foreign Secretary, Lord Palmerston, forbade British consuls "to afford the slightest countenance to religious agents," thanks partly to Don Jorge's flamboyant methods of evangelism. Settled near Lowestoft in Norfolk after marrying—not a luscious *andaluza* (for despite his robust physique Borrow may have been sexually impotent) but a naval officer's well-to-do widow—it was time to write the books which seethed in his mind. He remembered Spain as "one of the few countries in Europe where poverty is not insulted, and I may add where the wealthy are not blindly idolized...

The duke or marquis can scarcely entertain a very overween-ing opinion of his consequence as he finds no one, with perhaps the exception of his French valet, to fawn upon him."

He recalled the people of down-at-heel El Ferrol "boasting that the town contains a better public walk than Madrid, of whose Prado they speak in terms of unmitigated contempt"; approvingly reported the remark of a *posadero* in Muros ("an Asturian is fit company for a king and is often of better blood"); and quoted a Catalan living near Toledo who, offering water to drink, had commented that "it is cool, but the water of Castile is not like that of Catalonia."

But Seville released the fullest grandiloquent flow. "Cold, cold must be the heart which can remain insensible to the beauties of this magic scene... I have shed tears of rapture whilst I beheld it."

Borrow and Ford corresponded (in 1846 Don Jorge wrote announcing the death of Sidi Habismilk, who had been the wonder of the Norfolk countryside) and occasionally met. Neither revisited Spain. Ford may have been influenced by the memory of his new-born son's death in the Alhambra, and of his attractive wife's flirtation (perhaps more) with the French painter Eugene Delacroix, who did a portrait of her while Ford was away on one of his tours. The Fords sep-arated on their return to England and after Harriet's death in 1837 Richard remarried.

Nevertheless he was thoroughly Hispanified. He wrote long, learned articles about bullfighting and was an acknowledged expert on the art of Velazquez. He terraced the grounds of his mansion near Exeter in the Spanish style, building a Moorish tower ("prettier than the Puerta del Vino of the Alhambra") and installing a choice Alhambran fragment in his bathroom. Wearing his sheepskin riding jacket he wrote the *Handbook* and *Gatherings* in a pavilion shaded by cypresses imported from what he called "the most romantic, racy, and peculiar country of Europe." But in his lifetime the railway, so detested by Ford and by his hero the Iron Duke ("it will," growled Wellington, "encourage the lower classes to move about"), crept further and further into Spain—and with it a new breed of tourists who fancied the idea of "comfortable scurry."

VI

THE TRAIN IN SPAIN

A 19th-century tourist boom

Writing in the Quarterly Review
Richard Ford marvelled that Spain, "though a land of adventures and
romance full of historic, poetic and legendary association, yet is withal
a kind of *terra incognita* where the all-wandering foot of the all-per-
vading Englishman but seldom rambles. The beef-steak and the
tea-kettle which infallibly mark the progress of John Bull are as yet
unknown in the *ventas* and *posadas* of the Peninsula."

But he and Washington Irving, Gautier and Dumas had done
much to ensure that Spain experienced her first tourist boom, facilitated
by the locomotive and concentrated on Andalusia, with Granada as the
prime attraction. William Clark, a vacationing Cambridge don,
reported in 1849 that Mateo Jimenez, busy exploiting his fame as
Irving's guide, was a tedious old bore, "recklessly confounding dates
and facts, and for any special absurdity audaciously appealing to the
authority of "Vasendon Eerveen." Another guide, Immanuel Bensaken,
highly recommended by Ford (who had invited travellers' comments
for revised editions of the *Handbook*), was in 1856 described by an irate
Englishman as "making a practice of robbing tourists in every possible
way, charging them enormously for everything he helps them to purchase, being in agreement with certain shopkeepers."

In a note to Murray, Ford defended Bensaken: "a better bred
or more intelligent fellow will surely not be met with in Andalusia; as
to his being pouched by tradespeople to whom he brings customers,

this is so Continental and so Spanish that it amounts to a matter of course."

But this, according to Clark, was not the only problem. Rivalry between guides sometimes erupted in lethal brawls. Mateo Jimenez's son had stabbed a man for insulting his "venerable" father, who commented, "It was for this, just for killing a man when his blood was up, that they put *mi chico* in prison, *pobrecito*." Worse, foreigners were at risk. An English tourist had been threatened by three thugs who "drawing their knives, demanded his watch and his money... He immediately went to the police, and two of the men, whom he identified, were condemned to twelve years' imprisonment; an instance of summary justice which astonished the good folk of Granada, who complained, perhaps with reason, that a native would not have met with such speedy redress."

Inmates of the picturesque zoo could be troublesome. In the 1870s Augustus Hare, a prolific "topographical writer," was disgusted by "the savage insolence of the gypsy population, their coarse language and manners and their brutal immoralities... If an English lady ventures into the gypsy quarter alone, a troop of young women and children will not scruple to fall upon her, and while some carry off her shawl, parasol etc, others will force their hands into her pockets." Outside the Sacromonte caves "the children who are not busy begging roll in the dust, often quite naked and without distinction of sex."

The Italian Edmondo de Amicis wished he had not ventured into territory peopled with savages "inaccessible to the police, shut to those who take the census, ignorant of every law or government... with a language and customs of their own, false, thievish, mischievous and murderous." Surrounded by half-naked, emaciated creatures and forced to buy them off, he felt lucky, he said, to escape with his life. Wild, insanitary gypsies were not the only Andalusian hazards. Believing that cleanliness was next to godliness, the wife of an English clergyman, seeking lodgings in Málaga, was astounded when a landlady, summoned to explain the presence of a bed-bug, laughed contemptuously, exclaiming "*¡Si fuese un toro!*" (If it had been a bull!)

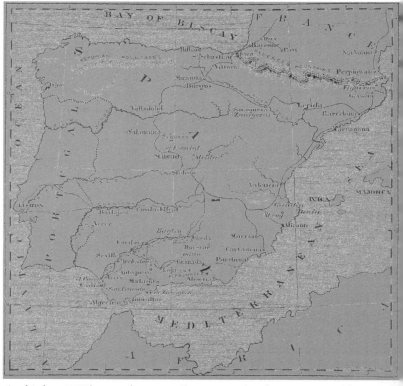

As this late 1870's map shows, a railway network, often constructed by British engineers, had facilitated a minor tourist boom.

Rev. Hugh Rose, chaplain to European mining communities in Linares and later English chaplain in Jerez and Cadiz, had little sympathy for tourists who "make no attempt to see anything beyond the stock sights at Seville or Granada, exhibited by flippant, exorbitant and ignorant English-speaking guides, most of whom are Gibraltar men—"rock scorpions" in fact. G. E. Street, who made a survey of Gothic church architecture, preferred to travel by road and risk a few *posada* fleas rather than use the railway, which by the early 1860s had "made it possible to travel from Calais to Alicante in an almost unbroken line." The cooking in northern *posadas*, he thought, was much better than in many English country inns. He did not go further south than Toledo and Avila ("we have already been treated almost to surfeit with accounts of the Moorish remains at Granada, Seville, Cordoba etc.") and hinted that discerning tourists might do well to follow his example.

The ever-hovering threat of civil commotion continued to make Spain a risky destination, as de Amicis discovered in 1872. Amadeo of Savoy was precariously king, but republican sentiment ran high, a second Carlist revolt had begun, war in Cuba was imminent, draft-dodgers took to the hills and turned bandits. In a café in Zaragoza he heard a shopkeeper demanding a federal republic without delay, together with "the shooting of several leading politicians in order to convince such crooks that *one cannot joke with the Spanish people.*"

Newspapers were full of sensational stories that Italy and Germany intended to attack France and Spain "for the purpose of destroying the Catholic religion." De Amicis quotes a typical outburst: "Let them come! We are still the Spain of 1808. The conquerors of Napoleon fear neither the grimaces of Emperor William's Uhlans nor Victor Emanuel's sharpshooters." The unfortunate Amadeo was described as "the poor child, the Italian army as a troupe of ballet dancers, Italians in Spain were invited to leave with the hardly courteous warning: "Italians to the train!" Itineraries were liable to be disrupted. Hare was peeved when "the railway to Asturias was cut in twenty-five places and we were compelled to give up visiting that most interesting corner of Spain."

Yet the number of visitors was increasing. Rev. Samuel Manning, an evangelical parson who combined tract distribution with journalism, reported that "old residents and tourists are beginning to complain of the invasion of the northern hordes. English and American travellers may now be met with not only in such places as Granada and Seville, but in Segovia or Ronda or Avila. And books of Spanish travel have multiplied in proportion." Hare, a stickler for propriety, deplored the behaviour of sightseers who walked and chattered around churches during services. In the Escorial Havelock Ellis, an eminent sociologist who often visited Spain at the turn of the century, watched "a disconcerting little stream of cosmopolitan tourists... Gaily dressed ladies from every clime... The patient Yankee globe-trotter, the smug English curate, the irrepressibly cheerful little Frenchman who stands in the middle of the solemn vault of the dead kings and sums up his impressions: "*C'est joli, ca!*"

Whatever their nationality, most tourists expected to watch at least one corrida. For as William Clark put it, "the first questions a traveller should expect on returning from Spain are "Have you seen a bullfight and have you encountered a bandit?" Sometimes a country clergyman will inquire whether you have been present at an *auto de fé*. As the two latter are out of fashion just now, a bullfight is *par excellence*, the thing of Spain." So with whatever real or assumed horror, writers had to tackle the subject. Their usual reaction, combining moral indignation and fearful curiosity, worked as a powerful inducement, enabling samplers to sit guiltlessly through even the nasty parts, forearmed as they were with suitably damning sentiments. Clark, however, though humouring, or titillating, Victorian readers boldly revealed himself as an enthusiast whose fervour, like that of Gautier, heralds the elaborate eulogies of such later addicts as Montherlant, Hemingway, Marguerite Steen and Kenneth Tynan.

"The masses," he begins, "already predisposed, like their brethren of the East, to hold life cheap, are at the corrida familiarized with the sight of blood; and this, I cannot doubt, contributes to the frequency of assassinations. A streaming wound, so far from chilling an Andalusian with horror, recalls the hours of intense enjoyment in the bull-ring." But Clark confesses that in Madrid and in Málaga, swayed by mob emotion, he had felt "a kind of savage joy indicative of the wild beast within, which we bridle with texts of religion and cram with scraps of morality." His sympathy had veered from bull and horse to matador, and he now believed that if Britons could forget their humanitarian hypocrisy they would experience a cathartic release:

"Before you have been half-an-hour in the arena," he promised, "you will watch the various chances of the fight with as much pitiless enthusiasm as if the northern star had never shone on your cradle."

De Amicis also refused to condemn the corrida. Having witnessed a cockfight in a pit holding over a thousand spectators, he comments: "I had no idea of such ferocious cruelty... Should you go to Spain, take my advice: be content, humane people, with the sight of the bulls." Especially since winter, Sunday shows in Madrid were likely to feature a piquant novelty: *toreras* "dressed like tight-rope dancers... The *espada* I saw was an old woman of 60 called La Martina, an Asturian known in all the circuses of Spain. These poor, unfortunate women risk their lives for 40 lire. When I was there a bull broke the arm of one of the *banderilleras* and so tore the shirt of another that she was left in the middle of the arena with scarcely enough clothing to cover her decently."

Rev. Manning concentrates on the fate of the horses, "staggering about the arena, their entrails hanging out... whilst the crowd yelled its fierce delight... a handful of tow may be thrust into the gaping wound to stanch the blood and protract for a few minutes its wretched life." But sad to say, even in non-Spaniards the first fine revulsion soon tended to wear off. "Not a few Englishmen resident in Spain have overcome their natural repugnance and visit the *corrida* as often as opportunity offers." Rev. Rose, on the other hand, optimistically announced that "one of the brightest signs of real, honest social advancement in Southern Spain is the desertion of the bullring; and the pouring in, like a slow flood, of all sorts of manly exercises. In Cadiz and Seville, in Port St. Mary and Jerez, horse-racing, boat-racing, and above all cricket matches, are now very common. And let me say, the finest fielders are Spaniards. A Spaniard rarely misses a 'catch.'"

Two formidable Englishwomen, Matilda Betham-Edwards and Mrs William Pitt Byrne, had seen no such hopeful signs. "I feel in duty bound," wrote the former, "to say a word about the bullfights, though I never recur to the subject without repugnance." She had been told that many educated Spaniards deplored the barbaric spectacle and that it was going out of fashion. But not only was the *fiesta nacional* flourishing, "Spanish ladies take their young children, who clap their hands at the close of every bloody act." And, final blasphemy, these odious events were blessed by priests and the profits used to build hospitals and churches—churches where the gory images of martyrdom reminded her of the shambles of the arena.

To judge fairly of such "horrid amusements," she said, it was necessary to go behind the scenes. "There, in a dreary chapel, you see the *matadors*, the *banderilleros*, and all the other wretched actors, taken by turns to confess and receive absolution... How ghastly pale and craven they look in their tinselly dresses! More like culprits going to execution than the proud heroes of great feats."

To Mrs Byrne, a militant civilizer, it seemed incredible that the bullfight should not have joined the Inquisition in merciful oblivion. But since a *gran fiesta* was "essentially a *cosa de España*," she felt that it must be seen. But the sight of a bull "with coagulated blood hanging like a broad crimson sheet from either side of his neck, his parched tongue lolling from his mouth," sickened her and her husband. "We felt but little concern for the toreros who went in for gain and for glory... We saw it, were utterly disgusted, and hope never to witness the horrid exhibition a second time." Henry Inglis had lamented that "a proposal to envelop the horses in a net, by which the most disgusting part of the exhibition would have been concealed, was a refinement which it was thought would not be relished by the mob." By the 1890s Havelock Ellis, though conceding that a bullfight had something of the character of "a sacred ritual," and that "the fact that the would-be slayer may himself be slain adds an element of dignity wanting in nearly every other form of European blood-sport," argued that it was nevertheless an anachronism. He therefore rejoiced that "with the approval of many toreros, a movement has begun for the mitigation of the more offensive features." (In the 1920s the horses were given protective padding.)

Though 19th-century tourists were hardy, even heroic, compared with the packaged masses of the 1980s, they had not the time,

A Danish magazine caricature of Hans Andersen in Malaga with a gypsy chestnut-vendor, resembling one of the winsome waifs in his sentimental fables.

nor often the inclination, for more than a fleeting glimpse of the primitivism which had delighted Ford and Borrow. Hans Christian Andersen, a fairly typical bourgeois toe-dipper, gives an animated account of what it was like to travel through Spain in the early 1860s.

His thanksgiving for railways is almost hysterical. "We now fly on wings of steam past what is dull, get out and linger with what is beautiful—is that not magic?" But one still sometimes had to use a diligence, and the highlight of Andersen's journey to Barcelona was the fording of a river near Báscara: "A strong current, another coach ahead of us floundering in midstream... The *mayoral* decided to plunge in passengers, baggage and all... peasants came to our aid—some held on to the coach, some to the mules, and in front went the pilot who knew the ford... In the deepest place the water came up to their chests and we had to lift our feet to prevent them from getting wet."

At Gerona he was glad to transfer to a train, which "really did appear to be witchcraft to many an old señora, who crossed herself before setting foot on the steps, and again before sitting down in this devilish horseless carriage." He took a coastal steamer from Barcelona to Valencia, having been told of "a particular spot on the road where the mountain stream often took command. A few years ago an over-crowded diligence had completely disappeared, carried away by the rushing torrent to the open sea."

When the coach in which he might have travelled did arrive in Valencia he congratulated himself on his decision. "It was only a ghost of the diligence we had seen two days ago. The horses were dripping sweat, the passengers limped out like hospital patients. Their hair was matted with dust, which also lined each wrinkled face."

He had been reluctant to leave Barcelona, "the Paris of Spain." But at the Fonda del Cid in Valencia the grapes were "as big as plums, the melons melted on the tongue like snow, the wine was fiery and potent." Only one drawback: the September heat was overpowering. "Rush mats hanging over the balcony to keep out the sun made little difference. One sat and gasped for air, which the ladies tried to capture with their fans... Social life flowered up the walls from storey to storey." At Almansa, sweating in his tight frock coat, Andersen consoled himself with the thought that he had been "so thoroughly warmed through that he would be able to do without a stove during the long winter in the North," and like a thrifty housewife this wealthy author added, "What a saving that would be!"

His coach journey from Alicante to Murcia was gruelling. The landscape "looked as if it were laid out for robbery... Solitary buildings were few and far between, with cisterns to catch rainwater, which was sold by the glass, tepid and greyish. Mixed with anisette it tasted like medicine." The going was bumpy, "as if we were driving over an endless dried-up village pond." The diligence, pitching from side to side, "often gave a hop over a hummock which was very disturbing to one's insides! To the birds of the air it must have looked like a ship in a heavy swell." But the ordeal was made tolerable by the charms of "nutbrown" gypsy nymphets very different from the pale, flaxen-haired maidens of his own rather mawkish tales. In one wayside hovel among "huge dusty clumps of cacti" he saw "a girl of about twelve, but fully developed, a real Murillo beauty... scantily-dressed, doubtless because of the terrific heat. She had a juicy bunch of grapes in her hand... "Wine and Passion" could have been the caption for that Bacchanalian picture. We were indeed in a hot country!"

In Málaga the heat was tempered by sea breezes and there was cool English ale to drink at the Fonda del Oriente. Andersen strolled around a market in the waterless river bed ("horses and donkeys, pots and pans boiling over open fires, counters and tables set out"), and wandered dreamily in the Protestant cemetery founded in 1829 by William Mark, the British consul, to end the practice of burying heretic corpses in (as Richard Ford had said) "a hole in the sand." Here was "a paradise of myrtle hedges and tall geranium bushes. Passion flowers twined their tendrils over many a gravestone, there were pepper trees with weeping branches... and a friendly little house where one could get refreshments." Leaves, shade, headstones inscribed in Danish Dutch and German... this was more like home.

Then, remembering that in Copenhagen he had been solemnly warned that in Spain "travellers were constantly exposed to attacks from bandits," there was the excitement of being escorted by armed guards in the diligence en route to Granada. There had been a hold-up a few months earlier, "the only one in recent times." The brigands had not been hardened outlaws, but "peasants, a family whose youngest son had to do military service, and in order to get the money to buy him out they had taken to robbery." But nothing happened on this trip, and feeling almost cheated, Andersen "suddenly had a tremendous desire to experience just a little encounter with bandits."

Madrid, bitterly cold at the end of November, reminded him of "a camel that has fallen down in the desert." He cut short his cultural sightseeing and hurried back to Denmark. But his description of precociously mature gypsy girls probably made Scandinavian males think longingly of Andalusia. Edmondo de Amicis positively drooled

The port of Barcelona. In the 1860s the saying went that "Europe ends at the Pyrenees" because Spain was so different: but Hans Andersen described Barcelona as "the Paris of Spain ... in no country have I seen such excellent cafés."

over the southern belles. In Cordoba he is "bewitched by a golden-complexioned temptress with two lips that seemed to say 'Drink me' and two eyes that forced me to bite my lips to keep out of mischief." She seemed the epitome of what Andalusians meant by "salada, the word commonly used to convey that a woman is beautiful, graceful, languid, fiery, anything else in fact." Then came Seville, "the queen of Andalusia, the Spanish Athens, the mother of Murillo," and above all the city of *Sevillanas*. Could there be, anywhere, "women so fitted to suggest the idea of abduction, not only because they arouse the desire to commit all sorts of deviltries, but because they really seem created on purpose to be seized, bundled up and hidden away, so small, light, plump, elastic and soft are they. Their little feet could be got into your coat pocket, you could lift them by the waist as you would a doll."

Further inflamed by the sight of *cigarreras* at work ("800 dark heads of hair, 800 dusky faces from every province of Andalusia"), he claims to have developed an erotic fever culminating in a dream which drove him to beg the Italian consul "to take charge of me, for this city is frightening! I seemed in this dream to be tied to the bed by a long black braid, to feel on my lips a fiery mouth which took away my breath, and around my neck vigorous little hands were crushing my head against the neck of a guitar!"

Heading south for a less delirious but satisfying sip of Andalusia, Matilda Betham-Edwards journeyed in style, making full use of railway facilities. Her motto was "always travel in your best clothes and with half a dozen trunks at least. Luggage and good clothes ensure you good places, general civility and an infinity of minor comforts."

The ladies' *coupé* (first class) which she occupied was strewn with the paraphernalia of her proconsular progress. "A box of medicines, a folding india-rubber bath, a basket of provisions, two or three parcels of books, a leather bag of sketching materials... an odd bag containing notepaper, opera glasses, passports, a teapot, a water-bottle, an air-cushion... It is all very well for savages to travel light, but not a bit of our precious luggage could we have spared."

At Granada, having changed into a resplendent evening gown, she was in the mood to surrender to the seductive strains of a guitarrist from the Albaicin, performing "for a company of ladies and gentlemen whose utmost vagabondage had not exceeded boiling a picnic kettle in Epping Forest, or more likely taking tea on our own lawns. This was music one had never dreamed of. His fingers but touch the chords and your breath is taken away... You are indeed for the nonce a gypsy, your pulses are quickened to gypsy pitch, you are ready to make love and war. We felt thankful to Señor Antonio for having given us so full an experience of wild life in the space of a few minutes."

Mrs Byrne was not so easily beguiled. To her schoolmarmish mind Spain was largely a problem in collective delinquency. "Whenever the Spaniard is civilized," she fretted, "it will be in spite of himself. If the self-satisfied denizens of the Peninsula (a word which seems to imply disconnection from the civilized world) have submitted to the partial inroad of rail and steam, it is because the novelty has been thrust upon them by foreign enterprise." Eventually, though, even Spain would have to obey the inexorable law of Progress, but this would happen more quickly if Spaniards would more often travel abroad "to enlarge the borders of their understanding. They must be made conscious of their wants; they need, in fact, in full and active operation, the incentives of the Iron Age."

Yet, aware of the dark side of industrial revolution in Britain, Mrs Byrne paused briefly in her social engineer's tirade to "grieve that the simple, honest and noble peasantry of Spain are on the brink of such an abyss." She could only breathe a prayer that somehow Spain "would escape the blasting breath of the Iron Age unscathed."

The blasting breath of her particular prejudices was directed at an array of shortcomings. The bread would pass muster, but oil and garlic turned her stomach. Wines were mostly spoilt by "the pitchy taint of undressed goatskins. The Valdepeñas, which is thought so much of in England, is here rather inferior to liquorice tea, and Málaga has a physicky taste." But these were trifles compared with the prevailing sin of "inconsiderateness for the weaker sex" (hard to believe that Mrs Byrne numbered herself in this male-invented category). "Doubtless Oriental tradition has contributed to the notion that women are inferior animals subordinate to the wishes of her lord and master... Generally speaking they are just sufficiently trained to form useful domestic machines. They are never so well-dressed as their husbands, and their health and comfort is apparently far less studied than that of men."

Annoyed by the habit of staring and laughing at foreigners, she even suspects the motives of Spaniards eager to give directions and advice. "We fear," she tortuously speculates, "that the secret source of this anomalous civility is to be found in self-esteem and the desire to show off; the moment he fancies himself in any way superior his natural politeness rises to the surface, concealing for the time the unamiable arrogance in which he is apt to indulge."

But Mrs Byrne's choicest structures were aimed at smoking, spitting Spain, with its "tobacco-thickened atmosphere." She warns

Once a favourite rustic retreat for the Spanish court, the shady gardens of the
palace at Aranjuez made a pleasant excursion from Madrid.

her readers that "from the moment you cross the frontier you are in for
it. Until you fairly quit Spanish territory you must be content to be
poisoned morning, noon and night by the nauseating effluvium... Not
only the leaves of books but the very leaves of the trees, as you walk
along the *alamedas* which skirt the towns, exhale the unsavoury
fumes." Moving at home in social circles where a smoking-room was
set aside to spare the ladies, and men wore smoking-jackets, she was
appalled by "the selfishness of the Spaniard" in this respect. Could he
never exercise restraint? At San Sebastián she watched "ladies disport-
ing themselves like naiads on one side of the bay, while straw-hatted,
hirsute mermen dabbled about on the other, smoking cigarettes even
in the water."

When a Spaniard reluctantly removed a cigar or cigarette from
his mouth, he did so "only to spit; and this unattractive process he
repeats so frequently and with so little regard to the rules of decorum,
that it requires some skill to avoid defilement." Pavements, staircases
and floors (even when carpeted) were, she reports, "literally wet from

this cause." Madrid was peculiarly spittle-strewn, and in the cafés she noticed that "scouring is undreamed of; the custom is to sweep and then water them to lay the dust... But when one considers inhabitants who smoke incessantly and spit without intermission, till the aggregate result is almost equivalent to a shower of rain, we presume to think that a greater ablutionary remedy would be desirable."

Seville, to Mrs Byrne, seems to have been chiefly commendable for a relative sense of hygiene, her lodgings there being "far cleaner than any hitherto encountered. True, the chef does all his work with a cigar in his mouth and even the *mozos* scarcely remove theirs while they wait upon the guests; but this is a *cosa de España*," Highly polished, spittle-free parquet flooring was indeed "a refreshing sight after the unclean and begrimed *suelos* of the more northern provinces... Although there is not less smoking here than in Madrid, the different condition of floors and pavements is very striking and is a test of superior refinement which we record with satisfaction."

Augustus Hare, escorting a group of female tourists, is often as tetchy as Mrs Byrne. The dust and jolt of a diligence was, he thought, preferable to rail travel, for Spaniards "hate and abuse the railways and bring the trains as nearly as possible to the speed of the old mule traffic." Inns and hotels left much to be desired. At Manresa "the door opened into a stable, where a number of rough-looking men were drinking. No looking-glass, no washing-stand in the rooms, though when we remonstrated, a pie-dish was brought for the ladies." Another establishment to be avoided was "the wretched and only *posada* at Manzanares, which charges extortionately for a single egg." But the Hotel de Paris at Aranjuez was certainly "one of the worst tourist traps... An English lady with her two servants, waiting there between trains, found themselves locked in till they had consented to pay 230 reals for their luncheon and use of a room." Even in the cities Spaniards were often deplorably unsophisticated and unmannerly. In Valencia his ladies, lacking the mantilla which was still obligatory for women of social standing, were "followed, much as an Indian in feathers would be in Regent Street; and those who went to see Ribera's paintings at the Colegio Patriarca were forcibly ejected for venturing to enter in bonnets."

Rev. Manning is scarcely less critical. Having decided that it would be more accurate to say that "Europe ends at the Pyrenees" rather than, as the French did, that Africa begins there, he complains that in Madrid his sleep was constantly disturbed by street cries.

"Milk vendors, newspaper and lottery sellers, the *serenos*, who keep the echoes busy till morning... They say the hour and the state of the weather as our old nightwatchmen used to do... *Las dos y sereno* or las *cinco menos cuarto y lluvioso*." In Cordoba he notes an early example of Spanglish in the brochure of "the Rizzi Hotel, in the most centrick place... Yet also has ackney coach and hole of post office." Granada confirms his belief that "in the mind of the Spaniard religion and morality have little to do with each other." During a procession the crowds knelt and prayed loudly, but "some of the worshippers succeeded in picking the pockets of three of our party at the moment the Host was receiving their attention."

Spiritually and politically Spain seemed almost beyond redemption. "The iniquitous Inquisition crushed all freedom of thought and action... For three centuries Spain has suffered the penalties of slavish submission to Rome." But now that evil was being challenged by another, perhaps even worse—the anti-clerical atheism that was spreading among the masses as "federal Republicans threaten the disintegration of Spain into a cluster of semi-independent provinces. Repressive tyranny is rapidly passing over into a lawless anarchy." The remedy was clear: "The Gospel alone can rescue Spain from the degrading slavery of the past, yet preserve it from the licentious excesses of an infidel reaction... Thousands have thrown off the yoke of Rome and professed their adherence to Protestantism. In a sober, rational religious freedom there is yet hope for Spain."

Living in the bleak lead-mining town of Linares in the province of Jaen during the First Republic (1873-4) the Rev. Hugh Rose M.A. (Oxon) set down his impressions of that chaotic period. King Amadeo had abdicated, a federal republic had been proclaimed.

During the second Carlist War trains were sometimes held up and
robbed by Carlist guerrillas or bandit gangs. Augustus Hare
complained that "the railway to Asturias was cut and we were
compelled to give up visiting that most interesting corner of Spain."

But the provinces interpreted this to justify "cantonalism," disregard-
ing the government in Madrid and making their own little revolutions.
In Málaga, Rose watched militiamen celebrating the independence of
Seville and the rebels' seizure of the Spanish fleet at Cartagena. In
Linares, where much foreign capital was invested, vigilantes prepared
to resist attacks by rebels who had "ordered all nuns to leave their convents within 24 hours' and were extorting a "revolutionary tax" from
the rich. At "civil christenings" a brass band would "play Republican
tunes at the house of a newlyborn infant" while a party spokesman
"gave it some expressive name, as "Liberty," "Equality" and the like.
Navajas (clasp-knives), "some with blades a foot long, embellished

with the motto *Viva la República Democrática Federal*" were on sale. The night train to Madrid was held up and robbed. Then early in January 1874, with Linares garrisoned by civil guards, came news that General Pavia had dissolved the Cortes, firing a volley above the heads of the deputies (a coup technique imitated by Col. Tejero in February 1981). There followed a Bourbon restoration under Alfonso XII.

But despite the efforts of the *guardias* ("a fine body of men, the nearest approach to it in organization, perfection and military discipline, being found in the famous Irish Constabulary"), the atmosphere was that of a Wild West frontier zone. The Sierra Morena was full of brigands, often political refugees or men evading conscription for the war in Cuba or that against the Carlists ("we prefer to shoot deer"). "When they get an exceptionally "good haul," says Rose, "they will rig themselves out like *caballeros* and take a train to Seville or Madrid to enjoy themselves, then return to the hills, or stay in Madrid to become politicians.... Some, if their favourite government should come into power, would emerge at once from their hiding-place and accept office!"

Among the miners there was a fair sprinkling of refugees and of criminals on the run. In the damp of shafts deep-driven below the Phoenician and Roman workings, lead poisoning was common. Medical facilities were scant, a short life and a merry one was the general attitude, and Linares catered for it. "Every tenth house is a cheap wine venta. Houses of ill fame, alas, abound... and the gay banter, the brightly-lit rooms, and freedom of these unhappy homes seem to have a marvellous attraction for the poor, hard-worked pitman who spends most of his day at the end of some dark tunnel in a space six feet in height by four in width. Alcahuetas, or procuresses, wretched old woman, walk about to entice young girls from thirteen to sixteen into their evil dens... Mothers, forgetting natural affection, honour and duty, sit down quietly to chat with the vile mistress of the house while a young daughter is being seduced in the next room... Blasphemy is added to this unnatural crime. I have heard a woman, as she left her daughter in the embrace of some lewd debauchee, saying "*Vaya usted con Dios y con la Virgen!*"

Turkey-sellers in Madrid. The Rev Samuel Manning reported that
his slumbers were frequently disturbed by street cries: "milk vendors,
newspaper and lottery sellers, the *serenos* (nightwatchman) who
keep the echoes busy till morning."

At night in the cafés one was "half-deafened by the click of
dominoes; everyone plays and they are furnished *gratis* by the propri-
etor." Knife and gunfights ("usually over some wretched woman") were
frequent, though there was "far less drunkenness than in the streets of
any English mining town." Sentimental, scurrilous and bawdy ballads
and broadsheets were eagerly bought. The tale of two priests who,
changing parishes, swapped concubines, was, like other anti-clerical
concoctions, very popular. Rose pleads the ignorance and poverty of
many priests ("they often have to turn their hand to mending watches,
making bee-hives, hen-coops and the like"), and as a relatively broad-
minded Anglican he was ill at ease with some strict Methodists from
the tin mines of Cornwall who were employed as foremen at Linares.
"Captain Jack," a former lay preacher, was an example of a likeable
fellow warped by puritanism ("I was always glad when he laid aside the
"spiritual man," as he called it, and became once more the "natural
man" as he lit his short black clay pipe").

Rose saw the civil guards as his natural allies, champions of law and order doing their duty "whether tracking a gypsy horse-thief in the gray *campo*, quelling a popular insurrection, or superintending the extirpation of locusts" that, "hatched in the wastelands of Extremadura," swept over southern Spain like a recurrent plague in the 1870s. Thirty years later Havelock Ellis, summarizing the impact of the 19th century tourist boom, was inclined to think that it resembled a plague of northern-bred locusts nibbling away at the roots of a culture, or cultures, already under attack from progressive Spaniards.

No traveller would complain that "Spanish hotelkeepers are beginning to obtain their sanitary fittings from England, or that clerical and secular authorities alike are putting down the national vice of spitting" (one up to Mrs Byrne, perhaps?). But *flamenco* dancing and singing, itself a gypsy vulgarization of the *fandango* and the original *cante hondo*, was being relegated to music-halls or turned into a "show" without vital, expert audience participation. And it was depressing "to find cinematographic apparatus set up in the market places of even the remotest towns, and to hear the squeak of the gramophone where one once heard the haunting wail of the *malagueña*."

Even the *cigarreras* of Seville had, according to Ellis, become thoroughly respectable, "more so than the typical English factory girl and remote indeed from the insolent *cigarreras* of legend." In Granada "the exploitation of the stranger" had become "a more or less obtrusive industry." Washington Irving's picturesque tatterdemalions had been driven from the Alhambra, which had been turned into "a show-place, a carefully kept museum. Every year it grows more rejuvenated, and though the restoration is carried out with reverence, it is never beautiful to see in the aged the signs of artificial youth." How many other hitherto neglected treasures would suffer the same fate in the interests of the tourist trade?

VII

STIRRING SPAIN

The early 1900s

The 19th century closed in national disaster. The loss of Cuba, Puerto Rico and the Philippines stripped Spain of imperial pretensions except for the tiny enclaves of Ceuta and Melilla and a protectorate in part of Morocco. At the same time the rapid growth of the socialist and anarchist movements, themselves in hostile tension, was gathering to a point where mass revolt menaced Church and State. Revolutionary anarchism, with its hatred of centralized rule and party politics, had spread first and fast among the virtual serfs on the huge estates (*latifundios*) in the south; then, with the drift of peasants from Murcia and Andalusia to the factories of Barcelona, had migrated to what was soon to become known as Europe's most turbulent city.

In *Spain from Within* (1910) Rafael Shaw, an English freelance journalist based in Barcelona, produced one of the first serious attempts to interpret "the view of the mass of the nation—who unable, the immense majority of them, to read or write, are more inarticulate than their fellows in any country of Europe west of Russia."

He reported almost universal cynicism about the political system. Since the 1880s the two main parties, Conservatives and Liberals, had arranged to alternate in office, with the result that "dishonest governments were faced in sham battle by dishonest oppositions, and parliament, instead of being a public check upon abuses, is simply a facade behind which politicians can operate with impunity." Voting, nominally free, was controlled from Madrid by a network of caciques, "usually large employers of labour or money-lenders, on whom most of the working population depend for employment or to whom many are deeply in debt."

In Andalusia, bitterness at the rate of forced emigration—to Catalonia or to the former colonies in Latin America—had been deepened by government's failure to organize relief during the terrible famine of 1904. "People literally died of starvation, yet the clerical press in Madrid minimized and almost mocked at the suffering."

The Church, personified by the legendarily cunning and unscrupulous Jesuits, was thought to be the real power in the land, masterminding the tactics of reaction. Had it not instigated the anticlerical, antimilitarist "Red Week" riots of 1909 in Barcelona in order to have an excuse to close "blasphemous" anarchist schools and to tighten the Church's grip on education?

Yet there was a desperate shortage of schools and teachers, and "even people of good position frequently cannot write and spell correctly... There are, or were until quite recently, grandees who could not sign their names. Ignorance of the commonest facts of geography and history is astonishingly prevalent even in the middle classes." This might be attributed to a kind of perverse pride which scorned mere practicality, but among the masses there was often a hunger for knowledge as a weapon of liberation. "If a peasant can only pay for the schooling of one child, that child has to share his learning with the rest of the family." Shaw had known "lads of 14 who return after working from 6 a.m. to 6 p.m. in the fields to sit over the ABC and pot-hooks until they can keep their eyes open no longer, while their parents and brothers and sisters look on and encourage the student."

This clandestine struggle to "better themselves" was almost a religion with the more ambitious and politically conscious workers, contemptuous as they were of their alleged betters. *Individualismo* still ruled, the community as a whole was a rhetorical abstraction (an attitude summed up in the saying that "only fools and foreigners pay taxes"), so that anarchist cantonalism was the counterpart of upper class tribalism. Priests were specially despised for abusing the confessional to intimidate the ignorant ("so that the mistress might learn what the maid had been doing wrong"). Shaw suspected that "a pious cook once in my employ who fed her entire family at my expense may well have consulted her priest, and was probably told that it was meritorious to rob a heretic" (and in particular a trouble-making foreign journalist).

Conscription for the campaigns in Morocco, fought to save some shreds of "imperial" prestige, was made doubly odious by the continued sale of Bull of Crusade indulgences "first instituted during the reconquest to permit those who were fighting the infidel to keep up their strength by eating meat whenever they could get it." Inquiring into "the religion of the people," Shaw found it to be a curious compound of scepticism and naive superstition. Men would dismiss church-going as a female foible, and anyone known to confess regularly was treated with suspicion. "I don't allow my wife to go to confession," said a master mason, "and if she insisted I should refuse to provide for her. I'll have no traffic with the gentry of the long skirts in my family." Yet though purgatory and masses for the dead might be ridiculed as money-grubbing fables, there was a lingering belief that "there are always seven souls clinging to the cloak of the Virgin—not the Virgin on any altar but the real Virgin in heaven. They are all climbing up, one above the other, and by prayers and good works you can help the uppermost to get out and make room for the next."

It was widely asserted that thefts of church treasures, officially attributed to godless anarchists, were really carried out by priests who sold them to dealers or museums. And there was, says Shaw, a great sympathy for English-born Queen Victoria Eugenia. Had not the fake assassination attempt—a bomb thrown in the direction of the royal carriage on her wedding day, spattering her with the blood of innocent spectators—been arranged by Jesuits and Carlists to cast the blame on proletarian terrorists? Was she not disliked by the Jesuits because she might "introduce English ideas about the education of women" and, because of her Protestant upbringing, might open the eyes of Alfonso

Barcelona's "Red" or "Tragic Week" of 1909, with its barricades and convent burnings in protest against military conscription and a repressive Church, was followed in 1917-23 by a wave of strikes and savage street fighting.

XIII to the tyranny of the Church? There was even a pathetic expectation that "England must surely do something for us now that our king has married the daughter of your king" (Edward VII, who was in fact her uncle).

The Church continued to give its blessing to what many working class militants as well as "cultivated and thoughtful Spaniards" considered a degrading sport or ritual, the corrida. And a university professor, himself educated in England, told Shaw that he was saddened by the see-it-once attitude of British tourists who were making the task of reform more difficult." "My students say to me, if they, whom you hold up to us as an example in so many ways, support the bullfight, there can be no reason why we should condemn it. And meanwhile your English ladies come out of the bullring and tell me that what they have seen there proves us to be a nation of barbarians."

Other Spaniards, representing a strong undertow of romantic isolationism, grieved that their country should be stirring in its long sleep. During the 1914-18 war, when Spain was neutral, John Dos Passos, an American student in Madrid, heard the novelist Ramón del Valle-Inclán passionately denounce the evils of Europeanization.

Madrid, 31 May 1906. The assassination attempt. by a bomb concealed in a bunch of flowers, on Alfonso XIII and Queen Ena in the Calle Mayor on their wedding day. Many spectators and escorting soldiers were killed or wounded.

Progress? "Merely an aping of crass commercialism." Better, in his view, "no education for the masses than education that would turn healthy peasants into puttyskinned merchants. Better a Spain swooning in her age-old apathy than a Spain awakened to the brutal trade war of modern life."

But Barcelona, benefiting from a wartime industrial boom which brought quick profits and a determination among workers to get a fairer slice of them, was about to explode in a long and bloody class war. Employed as a printer, Victor Serge, a libertarian who had been involved in the anarchist turmoil of pre-war Paris, saw how news of the Russian revolution excited anarchist and socialist militants with the dream of a workers' republic. "At the Café Espagnol on the Paralelo, near the horrible *barrio chino* whose mouldering alleys were full of half-naked girls lurking in doorways that gaped into hell-holes," he mingled with hotheads "arming for the approaching battle... They dealt out Browning revolvers and baited the anxious spies at the neighbouring table." In mid-July 1917 "squads of blue-overalled militants patrolled the town, hands on their guns... We used to pass the Guardia Civil on horseback with their black cocked hats and bearded faces." But the revolt sputtered and was easily doused, though Serge had to restrain "a young man, balancing in his hand a bomb wrapped in newspaper," who rushed towards the *guardias* shouting "I am a free man! Sons of whores!"

Unimpressed with the histrionics of would-be revolutionaries who "behaved like great big children," Serge departed to Petrograd. But in the postwar slump the struggle smouldered on. In five years more than 700 people died in a terrorist war between workers' and employers' *pistoleros*. In 1919 Dos Passos, by then a fledgling newspaperman, talked to an anarchist who had escaped from jail in Barcelona. He did not see much chance of a real revolution. "We are being buried under industrialism like the rest of Europe. Even our comrades are fast getting the bourgeois mentality... If we could only have captured the means of production when the system was young and weak we would have developed it slowly, made the machine the slave of man. Now it is a race as to whether Spain will be captured by communism or capitalism. In its soul it is still neither the one nor the other."

In Madrid fly-by-night governments trembled and dithered. Eduardo Dato was shot, the third prime minister in about twenty years to be assassinated, in reprisal for police brutality. The Army claimed to be the only guarantor of law and order, and in 1923 Primo de Rivera, the captain-general of Barcelona, set up a dictatorship with the support of Alfonso XIII. Millions of Spaniards were in a goodbye-to-all-that mood to match, and threaten, that of the romantic, foreign intellectuals who fled to Spain in the 1920s and 1930s.

VIII

GOODBYE TO ALL THAT

*Robert Graves, Gerald Brenan and
the Bloomsbury Set*

"So I went ahead, resolved never to make England my home again," wrote Robert Graves at the end of his autobiography, *Goodbye to All That*, the proofs of which he corrected in 1929 at Deya, his haven in Majorca. For him as for Gerald Brenan, who had migrated to Andalusia 10 years earlier, "all that" included the constrictions of a public school education, the grim experience of the Western Front, and British philistinism—the moral equivalent of the muddy, static squalor of the trenches.

The flight of writers, artists and bohemians to the sunny "pagan" south was a feature of the time. Cheap living was a powerful attraction and Spain, still alluringly "backward," began to appeal as a destination for those seeking a Rip Van Winkle land relatively uncontaminated by commercialism, industrialism and admass conformism.

Gertrude Stein, an avant-garde American writer and lesbian feminist based in Paris with her devoted companion Alice B. Toklas, played a notable part in steering Graves and Hemingway, among others, to Spain. Graves, who was escaping from the wreck of a stormy marriage, selected Majorca, which he later vehemently defended against the slurs of George Sand, because the island was said to have the best climate in Europe and because he could live there for a quarter of what it would cost in grossly overcrowded England ("its optimum

116

population being about eight million, as in Tudor times"). Above all he longed for a place where "town was still town" without a sprawl of suburbs, and where "country was country... and the horse plough not yet an anachronism."

Deya, a fishing village with about 400 inhabitants on the north-west coast near Valldemosa, gave him all he wanted as a background to his work—"sun, sea, mountains, spring-water, shady trees, no politics." Majorcans were "agriculturally still in the 18th century." In stony, sparsely irrigated soil, ancient olive trees miraculously survived. In a forest of evergreen oak, pigs rooted, charcoal burners toiled, wild cats and martens roamed. Here was paradise for technophobic escapists: "Painters, pianists, perverts, Buddhists, runaway couples, vegetarians—all went away a little dafter than they came."

The dictatorship of Primo de Rivera collapsed, Alfonso XIII went into exile, a Second Republic was proclaimed, the mainland vibrated with social and political tensions. But Majorcans were unaffected and Graves happily wrote poems and books. What did it matter that beef, butter and cows' milk were in short supply? There were good neighbours, good wine, brandy at three pesetas a bottle, a profusion of fresh fruit, cheap black tobacco, full domestic service for a shilling a day. The masons who built Graves' house worked a 10-hour day for 16 shillings a week. No cars could reach the cove, the beach was empty.

Among the pioneers of the British intelligentsia's Spanish fancy was an oddly-assorted couple. Ralph Partridge, ex-officer, Oxford undergraduate, protégé of the basically homosexual Lytton Strachey but himself a hearty womanizer; and another Strachey "captive," the fey, ambisexual painter Dora Carrington. Going to Spain in April 1919, they heralded a new type of traveller, the hiker and the real or make-believe tramp, a category which was to include such articulate picaroons as V.S. Pritchett, Walter Starkie, Jean Genet and Laurie Lee. Walking up to thirty miles a day, journeying from Cordoba to Seville and from Toledo to Madrid, their enthusiastic report encouraged the panjandrums of the Bloomsbury Group—Leonard and Virginia Woolf, even the neurotic,stay-at-home Lytton

Mallorca, In the 1920s and 1930s the island drew a mixed bag of northern escapists longing, like the poet-novelist Robert Graves, to say "Goodby to All That" in a pre-industrial paradise.

Strachey—to follow their example if not their footsteps. Spain, said Carrington, was superb, dramatic, primitive and paintworthy. "I have seen sights one hardly dreamt of, and people so beautiful that one quivered to look at them... and then those El Grecos..."

In April 1920 Partridge and Carrington persuaded their reluctant mentor to accompany them on their second trip. At the same time Osbert and Sacheverell Sitwell, who with their sister Edith were soon to form a literary clique to rival that of Bloomsbury, arrived in Spain, "a symbol of our newly-won independence," Osbert explains. "We had just left the army. I after seven years of it... a long ordeal by boredom and null agony." Even crossing the frontier was thrilling. Great mountains, towering clouds, spectacular shafts of sunlight, "women carrying pitchers to the wells, men with straw hats as big as wheels, hog-skins filled with wine... All possessed the indefinable tang of an ancient and historic country."

In Madrid "goats on their way to be milked still marched in small herds through the outer streets lined with shacks made of petrol tins." Struggling to reach Toledo for Holy Week, the Sitwells realized that in Spain towns were "divided from each other by stretches of time so immense as to dwarf any mere measurement in miles." In essence Toledo was "as far removed from the metropolis as the most obscure town in Andalusia." They were amazed by the sight of "whole companies of the infirm and cretinous, crawling along on boards, hopping, twitching," and fascinated by the *pasos* of the processions: "gigantic grotesques, often representing personages of whom the populace particularly disapprove, Pontius Pilate or Iscariot." One effigy, that of "Ana Bolena" (Anne Boleyn), commemorated "the resentment felt by the proud Castilians at the behaviour of King Henry VIII to Catherine of Aragon."

Watching the pageant, the Sitwells spotted across the street "the elongated form of Lytton Strachey... Well muffled as usual against the wind and accompanied by his faithful companion Carrington—who with fair hair and plump, pale face, added a more practical but still indubitably English-aesthetic note to the scene, he was regarding the various giants and giantesses with a mute and somewhat phlegmatic air of appreciation."

The Strachey *ménage á trois* was heading home in sombre mood after a strenuous itinerary which had taken them to Seville, Cordoba, Granada, and finally, at Partridge's insistence, to the house rented by Gerald Brenan in Yegen, a village in the Alpujarras. Strachey, travelling first class while his attendants went third, complained that "all train journeys last for twelve hours at a minimum" and shrank from contact with non-Bloomsbury humanity ("the carriage blocked with smelly babies and drunken commercial travellers"). He rallied sufficiently to enjoy evening Mass in Cordoba, "a tenor singing an aria by Mozart... the pillars and arches of the antique mosque stretching away into far distant darkness... incredibly theatrical and romantic and I felt very nearly a Roman Catholic."

Granada he thought "astounding... Before long one observes picture-postcard elements, and the detail of the Alhambra is sheer Earls Court, but the general grandeur of situation and outline remain."

Soon, however, he was in a state of near-collapse caused, he suspected, by crude olive oil, greasy *tortillas* and a surfeit of *bacalao*. The prospect of ascending to Yegen by mule, the only means of transport in those days, appalled him. But Partridge, who had become close friends with Brenan in the army during the war, was determined to show off Carrington and the peevish literary lion.

Fortified with coñac after a bone-rattling bus ride to Lanjaron ("the roads, *ma chére*, the roads"), Strachey mounted a mule at Orgiva, but turned back when the animal plunged to the girth in the swirling springflood waters of the Rio Grande. Partridge and Carrington started to quarrel; Brenan, weak with flu, was distracted, and to make matters worse Strachey, who suffered from piles, had to dismount frequently during the thirty-mile trek. It was proposed to break the journey in the *posada* at Cadiar, but he considered the accommodation impossibly basic. Groaning, he completed the ordeal side-saddle on a wet, dark night.

The next few days were spent preparing the shattered littérateur for the return trip. "I shan't be sorry when this section of our trip is over and we return to comparative civilization," he wrote, though adding that he had never seen "country on so vast a scale—wild, violent, spectacular—enormous mountains, desperate chasms—colours everywhere of deep orange and brilliant green—a wonderful place, but easier to get to with a finger on a map than in reality!" It was an experience he did not repeat, and when in 1923 the Woolfs announced their intention of going to Yegen, Strachey did his best to dissuade them. "Spain," he warned in a falsetto squeak, "is absolute death."

Made of sterner stuff despite her ethereal looks, Virginia Woolf enjoyed her visit, "scrambling on the hillside among the fig trees and olives... as excited as a schoolgirl on holiday." But there was a lot of talking. "Gerald," she said in a letter to the art critic Roger Fry, "is very nice. We discuss literature twelve hours every day." Other visitors were to include Augustus John, Bertrand Russell and David Garnett, all prepared to endure the unpredictable cooking of "Black Maria," Brenan's temperamental housekeeper, and an unusual loo (described by Frances Partridge as "a draughty hole above a precipice").

During the six years he spent at Yegen between 1920 and 1934 Brenan, ultimately to rank with Ford as an interpreter of the Spanish scene, was busy at his books in a marathon of self-education, and making the detailed notes which were used in *South from Granada* and *Personal Record*. With his officer's gratuity he had bought and transported a Home University Library of some 2,000 volumes. Since only a handful of the thousand-or-so inhabitants of Yegen could read or write, the shy, lanky stranger was a figure of exotic peculiarity.

The village was not immediately attractive. Flatroofed, unwhitewashed buildings (not until some years later did Primo de Rivera decree that all Andalusian villages should be whitewashed to prettify their poverty). No doctor. No electricity or telephone. Only two houses with glazed windows. A sensation that the rest of Spain, the rest of the world, did not really exist.

It was assumed that Brenan had been fighting against the Moors, for were not all wars against the Moors? Foreigners were firmly stereotyped. "The Englishman had the reputation of being interested in mines and of having remarkable sexual powers. The Frenchman was a person who in a fight could always be defeated hands down by a Spaniard." Conversation was severely limited, schooling minimal. Of what avail was book learning in this primitive, self-sufficient enclave?

But there were compensations. The rent of the large, rambling house was a mere 120 pesetas (£6.00) a year. Scandalized by Brenan's efforts to shop, cook and fetch well-water himself, the village women found him a housekeeper. Maria turned out to be a mixed blessing, but her services cost only one peseta a day.

Revisiting Yegen in December 1923 Carrington found Brenan very much at home. Writing to Strachey, she described a musical evening. "Two guitars and a lutta... Gerald took round the drinks... As his sight is poor and the light was rather dim, he invariably overfilled the glass or poured the anis on the floor. The villagers laugh at him whatever he does and the girls spent their time trying to make him

Robert Graves, the English poet who arrived in Mallorca in 1929
and was treated like a local squire in the fishing village of
Deya where he made his home.

dance or sing." Why, she wondered, would people choose to eat breakfast in cold rooms in England when they could "bask in the sun,
munch toast and cherry jam on a roof gazing on the sea and the green
mountains of Africa?" And who would bother to go to parties in
Chelsea when they could "sit by a log fire and watch the dancers of the
Alpujarras and hear exquisite shepherds sing ravishing *coplas*?"

She set up her easel and painted, and there were bookish
evenings. "Last night Gerald read Crashaw and Collins, and then Eliot
and Joyce, to me while Ralph slept in the rocking chair by the fire."
But her host (and secret lover) also revealed a practical streak in
bargain-hunting forays, as on "a frenzied afternoon at Mechina. We've
bought masses of plates and jugs, a Kashmir shawl, a tablecloth, two
striped rugs and a carpet... We now contemplate a crate of china from
Almeria to Tidmarsh" (Strachey's house near Pangbourne in
Berkshire). The villagers had fallen over themselves to sell what they

thought of as worthless junk. "Old hags, young women, fat monsters, old men, half-witted men, all running out of their dens laden with jugs etc and surrounding us with shouts in the street. The bargaining was terrible, Gerald and Ralph of course were masters at it..."

More intimately involved in pueblo life than any previous foreigner of his kind, Brenan had come to feel affection for Yegen and "beyond it the yellow, ox-hide land." Rebelling against the conventional values of his parents and of his school (Radley), scarred by "years of boredom in base camps and trenches" alternating with such traumatic chores as shovelling corpses into mass graves during the battle of the Somme ("heads came off at a touch, horrible liquids oozed from the cavities"), he appreciated the "certain modicum of anarchy and non-compliance" he found in Spain. Here, he thought, was "a society which puts the deeper needs of human nature before the technical organization required to provide a higher standard of living... a land that nourishes at the same time the sense for poetry and the sense for reality, and neither of these accords with the utilitarian outlook."

Yet he had felt no special pull towards Spain, having considered Greece and Italy after discarding plans to live among the Tuareg in the Sahara. In a train crawling across the central plateau he was depressed by "the emptiness and monotony of the country." In Madrid it rained heavily and in Granada he "saw the Alhambra in a steady drizzle... shoddy and bedraggled, like a gipsy girl sitting under a damp hedge." His first impression of Spaniards was of a "glum, short-legged race who hurried past under umbrellas or else talked in loud, raucous voices till two in the morning."

In that autumn of 1919, plagued by dysentery, bitten by bedbugs, unable to afford medical treatment, he tramped the mule-tracks of Andalusia ankle-deep in mud (none of the roads had yet been surfaced) in search of somewhere to settle. It was a fearful initiation, yet an incident along the way encouraged him to persevere. In a cavernous parador at Ventas de Huelma a large dish of rice and bacalao was produced, and "each man, keeping his hat firmly on his head in the manner of a Spanish grandee asserting his equality to everyone present and to come, chose his section of the bowl, and after inviting myself and the others to do the same, dipped his spoon in it with great formality... He continued eating till the partition that divided his section from his neighbours had worn thin, when he laid down his spoon and as soon as the others had done so too, got up and washed it at the pitcher and returned it to the *faja* or red flannel waistband where he usually carried it. For the first time since I had landed, my heart warmed to the people of this country, who in such an admirable way combined simplicity with good manners."

The Yegen house came as a godsend. Omnivorous reading (he had vowed to "learn something about philosophy" and to teach himself Greek), insatiable curiosity, keen intelligence, and heroic pedestrianism—sixty miles in twenty hours over the sierra from Granada, for instance—combined to make him a resident-roamer of unusual range. His friend V.S. Pritchett was to call him "an encyclopaedia with wings," and Brenan's scholarly equipment, vitalized with imaginative insight, grew to rival that of the Italianate Norman Douglas as displayed on *Old Calabria* and *South Wind*.

Immersed in ancient history—"reading Virgil and working through the twelve volumes of Frazer's Golden Bough and the Old Testament"—the antiquated farm gear ("the sickle was identical in form with those found in Bronze Age tombs near Almeria") delighted him. So did the moment when, examining the change given in the village shop when he bought some cigarettes, he realized that some of the coins were more than 2,000 years old, among the first to be minted in Spain. They had been recirculated by a family who, inheriting them as a legacy but being unaware of their value, had decided to spend them.

Nor was diversion lacking. Yegen offered a rich sequence of pagan-Catholic festivals, a dance in one house or another most nights of the week, *sabias* (wise women), witches white and black, *curanderas* (healers), two or three prostitutes (price: two eggs), strolling players who performed in a stable, snarling wolves in cages brought by trappers from the sierra. On fine nights groups of young men would serenade the girls they fancied. If welcomed they would sing a complimentary *opla*, if not, a satirical one. Similarly, on Midsummer Eve youths would decorate their girls' houses during the night with branches, flowers and bunches of cherries; but if they had quarrelled with them they would put up thorns and nettles."

Alpujarreños expected their priests to have a concubine, since that way "many people felt easier in their minds when their daughters went to confession." The men might smoke in church during mass, but even among nominally godless anarchists the cult of the local Virgin persisted. There was an arsenal of magic or superstition to hand. In some villages a priest certified to be "virgin" was called in to exorcise or deflect a potentially crop-damaging storm. Snail gatherers sang a traditional "charming" song when they searched the fields with lanterns by night. Incest was reputed to be a cure for madness, and one father copulated with his daughter in the hope of ending her attacks of nymphomania. A nephew of Lytton Strachey, staying with Brenan, was seized by gypsies while wandering alone, having been taken for a *sacamanteca* (a wilderness-haunting ghoul said to feed on human fat) and hauled before the mayor of Yatar.

Long experience of grinding poverty had "made any sort of eating an act of daring and extravagance." Old women especially "developed a sort of prudery about it that in other countries they developed about sex." In some families each member would prepare his own food and "eat it at a separate table with his back to the others." For the very poor there was comfort in the thought of death, the great leveller, and the cemetery was known as "the *tierra de la verdad* or place of truth."

Sometimes ballad hawkers would appear, selling tales of miracle, murder and brigandage, for in the early 1920s out-of-work shepherds sometimes robbed travellers in the mountain passes. At 4,000 feet above sea level winters were cold, and such events would be discussed round the *mesa camilla*, a circular table with a brazier of wood ash or charcoal beneath it and a cloth that hung to the floor and was divided into "skirts" for greater warmth. Blissful for engaged couples, who "could hold hands for hours" without being seen, but, since the brazier emitted stupefying fumes, "undesirable for anyone who did not wish to be stupefied."

Brenan, who preferred an open-hearth fire of oak logs, gorse clumps, or aromatically fragrant lavender and cistus, speculates that the *mesa camilla* was perhaps a cause of the steep decline of Spain in the 17th century. "The forests were cut down... family life grew denser, more orientally bourgeois: reading ceased in the prim harem atmosphere... Spain became the classic land of stagnation." And in Andalusian households the man became "a constitutional monarch in a government of women... he is waited on hand and foot, but his advice, if he ventures to offer any, is disregarded."

Because they were a symbol of dignity, and for fear of catching cold, hats were seldom removed until bedtime, though by the late 1920s tradition was being challenged by daringly hatless youths and girls in shorter skirts. Even Granada, apart from its trams and motor cars, was much as it had been a century before. Water-sellers were still in business, "ice-cream makers continued to fetch their snow on mule-back from the summits of the sierra just as they had been doing since Arab times."

At night *novios* were to be seen "pressed like moths against the bars of ground-floor windows," and Brenan himself experimentally courted a girl in Almeria. His hours of duty were from 7 to 9.30 and from 10 to midnight. "I gulped down my dinner," he writes, "to take up once again the task of making conversation through the bars of a window with a girl to whom I had absolutely nothing to say." He was fortunate not to have had to use a *gatera* (cat-hole), as was the custom in the provinces of Cadiz and Seville, where "one could see, in one of those long, empty streets of the country towns, dazzlingly white by moonlight, a row of cloaked and prostrate figures discoursing in whispers to their (also prostrate) *novias* within."

Watching the evening paseo in Almeria, the women's "dark, velvety eyes, their brown bodies thinly concealed by cotton frocks, their languishing glances and gestures," Brenan was roused to dream of erotic adventure. But he soon realized that "the more subversive the

Gerald Brenan, known for such classics as *South from Granada, The Spanish Labyrinth, The Literature of the Spanish People*, and *The Face of Spain*, seen here as a young man in Yegen in 1922

climate, the more carefully the women are hedged in, and the less opportunity there is for casual love affairs." In an anarchic land full of spoilt, irresponsible males mouthing revolution, the steady conservatism of women held things together. Outside marriage, only brothels or (if she could be afforded) a kept mistress catered for sensuality.

Restless in Yegen ("Oh God," he once wrote to Partridge, "to have a little money... To waste my whole youth, alone at Yegen, is more than I can bear"), Brenan sometimes visited brothels and cabarets in Almeria and Cordoba, but his favourite pleasure city was Seville. He felt as passionately about it as Havelock Ellis, who had described it as "the heart of Spain. Every Spaniard is proud of Seville and glad to go there; every woman is happy to be mistaken for a Sevillian." Brenan could "think of no greater happiness than to live here almost like a workman with a girl of the working classes, come every day to the café to write, and return to her in the evenings."

It was not to be. But in 1929 Don Geraldo was offered the "squireship" of Yegen on condition that he married the illegitimate daughter of Don Fadrique, his deceased landlord, and his increasingly troublesome housekeeper Maria. He declined the offer, preferring to take as mistress Juliana, a lusty 15-year-old village girl. It was a tremendous sensual binge, his "first and last passionately physical affair." But despite idyllic interludes ("whilst I read Pastor's History of the Popes, Juliana irons or sews") he was far from totally ensnared and was worried about the penalty for seducing a minor. His letters outlining a campaign to disentangle himself and to secure custody of the fruit of the affair—a baby girl—amazed his friend Partridge. "You are the final incarnation of Machiavelli," he commented. Since Brenan seemed uncertain that he was the father, Partridge added helpfully, "the length of the upper lip is the test feature to exclude Paco and the lorry-driver from paternity."

It was time, probably, to think of leaving Yegen. A Belgian engineer of Brenan's acquaintance, admiring the wholesomeness of the common people's traditional values, sensed danger and decadence in meddling with them ("in every attempt to raise their standard of life he saw the hand of Moscow"). But the long, heavy—to romantic outsiders, enchanted—slumber could not last for ever. In 1934, when a road linking Yegen to Granada was completed and the village became more accessible, Brenan, now married to Gamel Woolsey, an American writer, moved to Churriana, near Málaga, having gathered rich material for the first truly searching account of an "unspoilt" pueblo.

IX

BEAUTIFUL, BACKWARD SPAIN

The 1920s and the 1930s

Ford, who pictured Spain as an antiquarian's delight, had helped himself to bits and pieces of the crumbling Alhambra. But this and bargain-hunting forays like that described by Carrington pale into insignificance beside the vulturine operations of Arthur Byne, an American art expert who, as agent for the insanely acquisitive multi-millionaire William Randolph Hearst (the "Citizen Kane" of Orson Welles' film), smuggled out of Spain entire buildings of historic interest. Decorated by Primo de Rivera for "services to the Spanish nation," Byne bribed officials on a princely scale to make possible such coups as the relocation of the monastery of Santa Maria de Ovila near Sigüenza. Bought for a mere $444, it cost Hearst a total of nearly $500,000. Expenses included the construction of a branch railway line, wages and food for a hundred onsite workers, the numbering and listing of every stone, 1,500 crates, and the hiring of a fleet of cargo ships to carry the 3,000-ton load of "construction materials" from Valencia to America.

Byne's booty had its parallels among writers who plundered Spain to produce hasty, spicy concoctions very different from Brenan's long-maturing study in depth.

Early into print was Elinor Glyn, the best-selling romantic novelist, with a book whose gossip-column tone can be gauged from her opening remark ("Spain is such a quaint country!") and her reaction to the Alcazar in Seville: "What wonderful creatures those old Moors were!"

She was particularly taken with the grandness of High Society, unafraid to live in style. According to her "le *peuple* are not resentful at there being great families who have palaces, and it is not swagger and ostentation or *nouveau riche* to have a certain display, but just natural... You have all the time the sensation that you have gone back into another century, where you have not to *pretend* that you like democracy!" She saw nuns serving "a special omelette" to the king after High Mass on Easter Sunday, and learned of "a most interesting privilege (all these romantic things delight me!)" enjoyed by the Dukes of Hijar and Alioga. The story was that "in about 1200 or something an ancestor saved the then Spanish king by changing clothes with him and being killed in his stead, so on the birthday of all the kings ever since, every garment that the king wears on that day is given to this family. They have a special large room to keep them in... and it does look so quaint to see the present king's clothes from his first year onwards! Funny little sailor suits and tiny uniforms—even his baby shirts and socks!"

She felt sure that the beggars outside Toledo cathedral would have contributed their last mite to swell the Virgin's treasure: "However you look at it, as a bar to material progress or as proof of superstition and ignorance, it is very *beautiful*... If you can hardly read and write and live on the scantiest food, it must be good to have the certainty that beyond this earth you will be blessed."

Further reflections on the Spanish temperament occurred while taking tea with Queen Ena after a charity corrida. "Down below one could see primitive nature stamping and snorting, ready to kill us if the planks had given way!" This was "very like certain aspects of Spain. Always one feels the wild rush of untamed nature underneath, no matter how wonderful the art and the civilization may appear on the top, and this is what causes the wonderful fascination to me of everything Spanish."

More pretentious than Elinor Glyn's Letters was Virgin Spain, described by the American author, Waldo Frank, as "a Symphonic History." Its pseudopoetic mannerisms exasperate, and Hemingway rightly deplored the popular appeal of such "bedside mysticism... the whole thing is what I call erectile writing, full of pretty phallic images drawn in the manner of sentimental valentines."

But Hemingway wrote a good deal of purplish prose about Spain, and his celebrated *Death in the Afternoon* passage, explaining the role of emaciated horses in the corrida ("disembowellings, visceral incidents") as a burlesque prelude to the "tragedy" of the bull's death, could have been lifted from *Virgin Spain*: "The horse," writes Frank, "is the comedian of the drama. The bull tosses him. He lies on his back or, losing his saddle, plunges mad and blind around the ring, kicking his own intestines... This is farce."

Much of the repressed sensuality of Spaniards, he argues, is released by the corrida, for "the best efforts of Mérimée, Gautier and Byron have failed to make the Spanish man or woman in the least romantic. Spanish women have no instinct for the game of love. Sexual virtuosity is a slow process nurtured at the expense of maternal passion. The French or American woman's sexual science is an irrelevant perversion to the woman of Spain, who wears upon her head an invisible crown of matriarchal power." There were, he suggests, basically two kinds of women, "the mother and the prostitute. And both are mothers... the Spanish prostitute with the Cross lying between her breasts is the least mercenary, most womanly of her class."

Another American, the journalist Negley Farson ("I always reserved Spain for my emotional adventures") comments on "the abysmal propriety of Spain's night life" and of Spanish prostitutes, "sitting in postures of rectitude calculated to arouse the appetite of the don, who likes to feel that he has made a conquest." He claims to have met an American sailor in Bilbao who expressed his frustration at "the *paseo*, the continuous walk-around of young men and women under the arches that takes place in every city as the sun goes down. "They don't do anything!" he said. "They don't get anywhere!"

A friend in a Pyrenean village told Farson that the local priests "had fought the introduction of a motor bus line to the very last mile. Progress means roads, and buses mean that our young men will go to Pamplona, San Sebastian, Saragossa. They will see sophisticated people. And when they come back here, and the priest and the doctor and the others start at them again with their fairy tales, they'll tell those petty dictators to go chase themselves."

Nostalgic doubts lingered in Farson's mind: "Hacienda and hovel, pueblo and castle. Water drawn from the well, clothes washed in the stream, food cooked on the hearth, the silver tinkle of the mule bells of Spain—would factory chimneys better this?" But though he dreaded to think what progress might do to the land he loved, largely because it had not caught up, he was shocked by "the human scarecrows" he saw "walking about everywhere in Castile," and by the spectacle of agricultural labourers in Andalusia who, while he sat drowsing on a mule among blossoming almond trees, "were toiling in line with an overseer at the back... bent over, turning with their little heart-shaped hoes the baked earth... They were going to traverse that whole plain! Without machinery they would always be the prisoners of the land."

Some literary romantics were prisoners of their taurine obsession. Alban de Bricoule, the young hero of Henry de Montherlant's novel *The Bullfighters*, is virtually the author himself. Of an aristocratic family with Catalan origins, Montherlant had taken part in corridas in Spain while still in his teens. Wounded during the war, he returned to Spain and, as he said in an interview, "recommenced killing bulls until I was gored in 1925. My book is a study of the life of toreros mingled with the lyrical exaltation of the corrida considered as a survival of the ancient rites of sunworship."

Alban is hopelessly, deliriously hooked. "The truth was that he loved these animals too much to be able to go very long without killing them... Nothing was more fundamental than the need to murder when the murder was really creative." Study of the bull-centred cult of Mithras has revealed to him "the generation of love by combat, and the generation of abundant life by extermination, which was also personal regeneration in the sense in which the Apocalypse uses the words "washed in the blood of the Lamb" and St John writes: "The blood of Christ purifies us."

The perfect *faena* is "a long, tragic scrimmage between two

Ernest Hemingway, seen here at a *corrida* in the 1950s, claimed to have seen 1,500 bulls slain and criticized the Republican government for suggesting that "barbaric" bullfights should be abolished.

beings who had become one... a brutal and prolonged caress in which the boy brought the monster ever closer to him, just as one draws a woman closer when one is about to enter her flesh." But such rhapsodic sequences are balanced by flashes of bleak realism. Alban suddenly sees his *cuadrilla* as shabby "accomplices in murder." A veteran *picador* remarks that the worst enemies of a torero are VD and TB. "Women, the sweat going cold on you, too many iced drinks. If the bulls don't get you, these things will." The bull-breeding Duque de la Cuesta flays critics of the corrida. The English, for instance, who "show their "humanity" by refusing to treat a horse the way they would treat a Hindu." Anarchist ideologues, who "pretend to be shocked by the "massacre" of bulls in the rings... They are loud in the defence of horses in the arena, but the wouldn't object to packing it with people who don't share their ideas."

Hemingway's anti-anarchist bile in *For Whom the Besll Tolls* was perhaps partly due to the fact that these agitators stirred so much trouble on bull-breeding estates that there was sometimes a dearth of corridas. And interestingly, in view of his role as a Republican propagandist during the Civil War, Hemingway in 1931 characterized the newly-installed Republican government as a bunch of bureaucratic ninnies to intent on sucking up to the League of Nations softies that they had subsidized some newspapers to campaign for the abolition of bullfights. This was bad news for a man who, though badly wounded as a Red Cross worker in Italy, had been rejected for the army because of poor eyesight, and haunted *corridas* as a subsitute for the war he had missed out on as a soldier.

With typical *machismo* he regrets the depravity of Belmonte's "sculptural technique" which necessitated smaller, bred-down bulls for "degenerate" matadors elegant in their cape-play but, in his view, cowardly killers. He complains that of approximately 1,500 bulls he had seen slaughtered, only four had been dispatched by the *suerte de recibir* (that is, killed while advancing on the espada), said to have been a common event in the legendary Golden Age of the sport. However, half-bulls were better than none at all, and it was not unmanly or moronic to take an interest in the *fiesta nacional.* Why did most Andalusian peasants show such enthusiasm for the *corrida*" Not because they were brutally ignorant but because, being very poor and lacking "modern comforts," they were keenly aware of the presence of death and therefore took "an intelligent interest in it" as ritualized in the ring.

Roy Campbell, a South African born poet who in 1933 fled, with his wife and two young daughters, from the Camargue to escape creditors, was already a fervent *aficionado.* And his wife's love affair with Vita Sackville-West, a feminist writer with Bloomsbury connections, had filled him with hatred for highfalutin intellectuals. Idealizing "simple" peasants, excoriating the Age of Machines, dreaming of a quasifeudal Arcadia, he was a natural sucker for Romantic Spain, a caricature of the backward-is-beautiful Hispanophile. After working for a time as an unskilled peon in the bullring at Valencia, he eventually moved to Toledo where, boozing heavily and sporting a Cordoban hat in the Borrow style, he churned out "Mithraic" verse on the theme that "the administration of death to a beautiful animal is a sacred sort of rite."

Like Hemingway claimed to have been, Marguerite Steen was, before seeing any, "all against bullfights" and had planned to launch an attack on what, as an animal lover, she considered "a brutal, so-called sport." Like him she became a voluble enthusiast, grateful to The Sun Also Rises—"that flashy little novel"—for directing her to Spain, which after a few months she thought of as "the country half my own." Ex-dancer, ex-teacher, and when she arrived in Granada in 1933 a successful popular novelist, she was instantly captivated, absorbing local colour so rapidly that *Matador*, a bulky melodrama, was published the following year. Hugh Walpole hastened to congratulate her: "It's terrific! My dear—written straight off your ovaries!"

The Spanish impressions of Evelyn Waugh and of the Czech writer Karel Capek, both of whom briefly visited the country in 1929, at least offer relief from the intensities of the blood-and-sand brigade.

In Seville ("feminine lushness with a cross on its bosom") the iron-barred windows remind Capek of "bird-cages hanging on walls" or "stretched chords upon which your eyes strum an amorous refrain." He is lyrical about *mantillas*—"this garb which blends nunnery, harem and the veil of the beloved." *Romería* carts festooned with ribbons, stuffed with singing, castanet-clicking girls, and illuminated with fancy red lanterns had, for him, "the strange, voluptuous aspect of marriage-beds filled with females." And of *flamenco* dancing he writes: "Take a Highland fling, a cakewalk, a tango, a Cossack gopak, an Apache dance, a fit of frenzy, unconcealed lechery and other frantic movements, kindle them to a white heat and begin to batter them with castanets, shouting all the while; then the mixture would begin to twirl as this dance twirls."

Barcelona, too, was a heady city. Seen from the heights of Tibidabo it was "a rich city, as good as new, which rather flaunts its money, its industries, its shops and villas... an ostentatious and flamboyant place, like its fanciful architect Gaudi, who so feverishly elevated his soul heavenward in the pine-cone turrets of that vast cathedral torso, the Sagrada Familia." But at close quarters it took on a different aspect. Here people lived not in patios but in the streets, sitting on doorsteps, gossiping on pavements. "Perhaps." Capek reflected, "that is why it is so easy for a mob to form and street-fights to start."

Around the harbour and in the murky *barrio chino* were garish bars and dancings, "low haunts more dubious than Limehouse, a brothel district larger than that of Marseilles." The working class suburbs were full of "men with clenched fists in their pockets and rabid, defiant eyes... A cigarette clings to their lips and their caps are pulled down over their eyes... Take a sniff and you will discover that something is smouldering here." Even the wide, crowded *ramblas* at the centre of the city seemed designed not just "to ogle the girls" but "to start a revolution."

Evelyn Waugh, a prickly traveller, has a good word for Seville ("certainly one of the loveliest cities I have seen") and commends Gaudi's creations in Barcelona ("in his work is apotheosized all the writhing, bubbling, convoluting, convulsing soul of Art Nouveau"). He even suggests that the Sagrada Familia "should not be allowed to decay... It would be a graceful gesture on the part of someone who was a little wrong in the head to pay for its completion." But he damns Tibidabo—"a frightful hill laid out as a pleasure garden with a restaurant and *café*, a hall of slot machines, an unfinished oratory of fantastic design, and a Great Wheel."

Gibraltar gets some hard knocks ("like a great slab of cheese... I will not say that I did not know that any town could be so ugly... that would be to deny many bitter visits in the past to Colwyn Bay and Manchester; but it was a shock"). So does Málaga: "Very little to see or do... smells strongly of olive oil and excrement... In the cathedral a riotous group of begging choirboys, paralyzed old women, and a dull verger." As for the wine—"a species of dark, sweet sherry which I had drunk and disliked in England"—it tasted no better in Málaga ("very nasty").

This, however, was petulant pop-gunning beside the raking fire of the Italian cultural historian Mario Praz. In a closely reasoned

The Sagrada Familia c 1927. "The whole thing", wrote R. A. N. Dixon, "is a bewildering combination of parabolic arches and of spires, walls and roofs sprouting birds, biblical figures, and what could well be artichokes."

polemic he warns that "tourists who go to Spain dreaming of finding another Italy (the only country which never has and never will disappoint the traveller) invariably come back disillusioned;" for, he insists, the essence of Spain is "a grandiose, overwhelming monotony," carried at times to the point of genius as in Don Quixote and the gloomy mysticism of St John of the Cross. The Escorial, for instance, is "a perfect image of monotony... a monumental cribbage board." Bullfights are unutterably monotonous. So, he thinks, are Spanish cooking, Holy Week processions and Moorish architecture. Yet the Alhambra was still "the Mecca of Romanticism," and "the formula of Spanish blood, lust and death is still being retailed... the gory, furious bull, the dagger in the heart of Our Lady of Pain, the stiletto in the heart of Carmen. It is always the same joint hanging from different hooks in the romantic Spanish shambles." And for Praz, Montherlant's taurine mystagogy epitomized the "false Spain" which had become "the Davos of neurotic, sexually obsessed intellectuals."

Though not concerned to prove a brilliantly overstated thesis, V. S. Pritchett was not uncritical. He reached Spain in 1924 as the somewhat unlikely correspondent of the Christian Science Monitor. The train journey from the French border to Madrid took 18 hours. There were few surfaced roads and those often so bad that cars seldom used them. He was struck with "the large number of fat priests—I had not seen so many even in Ireland—smoking cigars and playing cards." Madrid still had little industry: "the place was packed with government employees, most of them obliged to do two or three jobs to keep alive. Delay was the only serious labour."

Visiting Seville during Semana Santa, he saw "*ganaderos* and owners of olive groves and their relatives, their trousers high on their enormous bellies, sitting stupefied by the sun in their clubs," while "the peasants lived in huts where rush walls were beginning to be replaced by the flattened petrol can." Anarchist puritanism was strong in the region and there was a theory that the Andalusian ideal was "to see how few one could make one's material wants, an inheritance perhaps of Arab or desert culture." Far from being open-handed, even wealthy Andalusians were "famous for their parsimony... a rich man like Belmonte was certainly very frugal."

A year later Pritchett spent his last £20 tramping across Spain from Badajoz to León. His account of the experience, much influenced by D.H. Lawrence's prose, is too full of self-conscious, superfine writing to be much more than a curiosity (Laurie Lee did the same sort of thing better). He just about managed his twenty miles a day; slept on stone floors in ventas; shared a pigsty with "some very clean piglets"; lived on eggs fried in rancid olive oil; and thought he was going to die after sharing a garlic-laden stew with some railway workers.

Next in the line of literary picaroons was a make-believe tramp who later became director of the British Institute in Madrid. In the summer vacation of 1931, complete with fiddle and suitably shabby clothes, Professor Walter Starkie left Trinity College, Dublin, and took to the Spanish road as a scholar gypsy. He loiters in the Basque country ("nearly as green as Ireland"), and in Fuenterrabia notes that Spain's characteristic smell is of "burning olive oil," its characteristic noise that of "romping, irrepressible children."

Veteran *pordioseros* (beggars) teach him the art of conjuring coins from people who were often desperately poor themselves, and he acquires a stout, iron-tipped stick for self-defence. At Ezquioga, where the Blessed Virgin is said to have appeared to a young girl, he witnesses mass hysteria. In Castile, even in small villages where women worked in the fields and "seated upon a wooden board studded with sharp stones, drove a mule round and round to crush the ears of corn on the threshing floors," he is often asked to play the Marseillaise. "The atmosphere of revolution still clings to that rousing song, and in Spain it became the symbol of the struggle for liberty."

Working the trains on occasion, Starkie describes the vagabond musicians, shellfish vendors, lottery ticket sellers, and plain beggars who invaded the carriages, "including a cripple who had lost both legs and was carried round on a tray." At Covarrubias near Burgos he learns of the local custom of "courting with a stick. When a youth falls in love he writes the name of his novia on his stick. Then at sundown he goes to her father's house and pushes it through the cat-hole." If, when he returns before sunrise next day, the stick has been pushed out, it means he is rejected. If not, he can call with his own father to reclaim it and fix a date for the wedding. In Madrid, browsing among the bookstalls, Starkie chuckles over such gems of gaudily-jacketed pornography as At a Village in La Mancha, which "consisted of a lustful Englishwoman's amatory adventures, related with a wealth of picaresque detail." But even more, he relishes the mordant political gossip of the puertasolinos in the café *tertulias* of the Calle de Alcala, concluding that "with the exception of Dublin, no city blasts so many reputations in an evening as Madrid does."

Jean Genet's less jolly picaresque saga tells of his adventures in

Capek's sketch of a *fandango*. "To kick aside the long train gracefully, to twirl like a top and stamp the heels, demands consummate skill... This dance spurts up miraculously from a froth of flounces and lace petticoats.

a homosexual hoodlum underworld. He says that "in this most miserable period" (1932-34) of his life, when "Spain was covered with its vermin, its beggars... who went to Andalusia because it is warm, to Catalonia because it is rich," the *barrio chino* and the Paralelo swarmed with male whores and their sinister pimps. "We sometimes slept six in a bed without sheets and at dawn we would go begging in the markets, for the housewives would give us a leek or a turnip rather than a coin." For him, the violence that followed a right-wing victory in the November 1933 elections was memorable for the destruction of "one of the dirtiest but most beloved pissoirs." This had been a favourite rendezvous with perverts, and a delegation of transvestite "Daughters of Shame" publicly mourned the disaster. "In shawls, mantillas, silk dresses and fitted jackets, they went to the site to place upon the rusty, stinking scrap-iron a bunch of red roses tied with a crepe veil."

Passengers off cruise ships, ashore for a few hours with their expensive cameras, were so intrigued by the picturesque squalor of the down-and-outs that they would scatter pesetas for poses. But seeking the sun down south, Genet, so tattered, he writes, that "the elegant poverty of the fishermen wounded my own," tramped miserably along the coast until he reached La Linea ("one big brothel"). With other vagabonds he carried his tin can to "the barbed wire of Gibraltar to pick up the leftovers of the English soldiers. At night I tried to sell myself to them, and succeeded, thanks to the darkness of the narrow streets."

Tourism was still a mere trickle, except in Madrid, Barcelona, Seville and Granada, where, as Pritchett said, there were "some more or less modern hotels." In 1935 Laurie Lee passed through San Pedro, Estepona, Marbella and Fuengirola—"salt-fish villages, thin-ribbed, sea-hating, cursing their place in the sun. At that time one could have bought the whole coast for a shilling."

At Tossa, in the same year, Nancy and Archie Johnstone boldly opened the first foreign-run hotel. The Tossans, already used to the feuds of a German refugee colony and the eccentricities of such regular visitors as Henri Matisse and Marc Chagall, were now entertained by the sight of British holidaymakers heading for the beach in clannish droves.

Andalusians were disgusted rather than entertained by the sottish behaviour of Malcolm Lowry, already fast, and it seemed almost wilfully, descending into the alcoholic depths described in Under the Volcano. Spending the spring of 1933 in Granada with friends who were supposed to be keeping an eye on him (his father was paying them to be "guardians"), he drank vast quantities of aguardiente at a peseta the glass, and soon became known as "*el borracho inglés.*" Staggering about the streets, he was followed by jeering, mimicking children and cautioned by guardias. His shameless loss of control shocked Granadinos of all ranks, for as Lowry's biographer Douglas Day puts it, the unwritten rule was that, though a man might drink heavily, "he must drink well" and walk steadily, since "*dignidad* is the crucial quality of manhood." Lowry, fat and flabby, made himself even more conspicuous, and further offended propriety, by wearing a fancy tengallon, tourist-type sombrero which he evidently imagined to be authentically Spanish.

Old Spanish hands, with the proprietorial attitude of self-styled pioneers, frowned on tripper tourism when it seemed to threaten "their" Spain. Hemingway grumbled at the padding of picadors' horses in deference to outsiders' susceptibilities ("the bullfight has not existed because of foreigners and tourists... and any steps to modify it to secure their approval is a step towards its complete suppression").

Marguerite Steen found "the degradation of the bullfight to a spectacle for tourists nauseating." Germans on conducted tours were, she said, "loathed for their arrogance," and as for Americans, "the men had one idea, to get drunk; the women one idea, to sleep with a bullfighter." Even less enamoured than Hemingway of the Republican government, which she saw as the enemy of tradition and aristocratic style, she was resentful that "her" Spain should be vulgarized by "Reds" just when she had discovered it as a vibrant alternative to the drabness of Britain in the trough of the Depression.

The Irish writer Kate O'Brien, who had a soft spot for Bilbao, where "Carlists" and "Cristinos" still ostracized each other, was depressed by the misery of Castilian villages ("a rubbish dump with a dog asleep on it. The village idiot, a cripple girl, a baby with ringworm, the other village idiot"): unbearably sad places, she thought, "if you carry a heart and not a blue book in your breast."

But she bristled at signs of encroaching modernity. Spanish girls in the paseo, "dressed to kill, painted and waved, chattering and giggling, linked together in fives and sixes," seemed to her insipid. Many were now peroxide blondes in imitation of Hollywood sex goddesses ("no race of women that I know of takes these matters of beauty culture with such unfortunate seriousness as does the Spanish"). And she noticed that by the 1930s some modest provincial hotels, hitherto gloriously unimproved, had "gone *moderno* with garish strip-lighting, a radio as big as a bathing hut, and paintings of Sevillian ladies."

But these were trivial concerns compared to the foreboding felt by John Dos Passos at a socialist rally held in a bullring at Santander. "Schoolchildren in white dresses with red bows sang the

Opened in 1929, the ambitious Iberoamerican exhibition, of which the Plaza de España (here seen) was the centrepiece, transformed Seville, as no doubt will the exhibition planned for 1992.

Internationale. Somebody opened a box of white pigeons with red ribbons round their necks. They were supposed to fly up into the empyrean to symbolize the reign of peace" and goodwill that was to come, but must have been in their boxes too long in the heat. They dropped to the ground and all through Don Fernando's speech one of them flopped helplessly about in the centre of the ring." It seemed like a portent; and so did "the hatred in the faces of the well-dressed people at café tables as they stared at the sweaty socialists straggling back from the rally with their picnic baskets and their bunting. If eyes had been machine guns not one of them would have survived that day."

After the Popular Front's victory in the February 1936 election Spain—or, as so often before, the Two (or more) Spains—lurched towards a show-down. Five months later Norman Lewis, who had begun his travelling in Spain in the early '30s, when "merely by leaving the main road you could plunge immediately into Europe's prehistoric past," was alarmed by the atmosphere in Seville. The upper class family with whom he and his wife were staying took them to dine at a fashionable restaurant outside the city, "an ancient coaching inn of great charm in a setting of featureless prairies of ripening wheat." A cruel game began as "peasants, largely women and children emaciated and in rags," furtively approached the vine-shaded tables upon which small piles of perros chicos (half-peseta pieces) had been placed. When they ventured to snatch up a coin the waiters "would scream abuse and slash at the beggars with whips." Yet they crept back.

The Lewises were told that it was high time to teach these people a lesson they would not forget, and that very soon a private army of landowners would be riding round the villages to deal with the Reds. One of the diners was "a *rejoneador* who had been spearing bulls in the ring at Seville only the Sunday before, and laughingly he referred to this as valuable practice."

In a matter of days what the historian Hugh Thomas has called "the bloody corrida of the Spanish people" was to begin. Lewis set off for England, driving through Extremadura, through "the Europe of the Dark Ages, ghostly and skin-and-bone poor, with weasels sunning themselves in the dirt road... and once in a while a grey, wall-eyed shack with no glass in the windows and the slates sliding off the roof." Near Ciudad Rodrigo the road was blocked by carts, and he was questioned by red arm-banded militiamen who "would have been interchangeable with the wretched peasants begging for ha'pence but for the dignity conferred by hunting rifles and fowling pieces." Their leader, an unshaven schoolmaster who looked like a bandit, boasted that they were ready "to deal with the Fascists."

In Tossa and in Almuñecar, where Laurie Lee was working as a musician-cum-odd-job-man in a small hotel run by a Swiss terrified that his business would be ruined, anarchists took control. In their house at Churriana the Brenans hid a hunted "Fascist." But it was hard to believe that the generals' coup was more than a passing spot of bother. In Tossa, the Johnstones told their guests that "the last revolution lasted five days." But the village priest was arrested and the church furnishings ceremonially bonfired on the beach. Consuls urged evacuation and British destroyers patrolled the coasts. Robert Graves and the Campbells were whisked away on H.M.S. Maine. Laurie Lee, amazed that a warship should have come to rescue "a couple of English tramps" (himself and an impecunious novelist), watched a swastika-marked airship nosing overhead. "To Spain, so backward and so long ignored, the nations of Europe were quietly gathering."

But the *patria chica* mentality lived on. In their empty hotel the Johnstones noted "the firm local belief that Franco is attacking Madrid only as a preliminary to his real objective, Tossa."

X

SPAIN UNDER FRANCO

The 1940s and 1950s

"In Spain," wrote V. S. Pritchett in the early 1950s, "we see life exposed to the skin. All the hungers are blankly stated there." Arthur Koestler, who in 1937 spent several months under sentence of death in Seville, had seen a country in which "the Moors were let loose behind the Pyrenees, this time as defenders of the Church. The shadows of the Middle Ages seemed to have come alive, the gargoyles were spouting blood, the air smelt of incense and burning flesh."

The Civil War had driven about half a million Spaniards into exile. Many towns were so battered as to be barely habitable. Prolonged drought and meagre harvests had brought famine. In overcrowded prisons and forced labour camps about 150,000 "Reds" perished or were executed between 1939 and 1943. In the 1940s sporadic guerrilla activity in Galicia, Asturias, Aragon and Andalusia failed to spark significant revolt from a terrorized population.

Until Cold War politics rescued Spain from total isolation as a minor, but still despised, ally of the Western democracies, it was a pariah nation. Driven in upon itself by a United Nations boycott, Spain seemed as inaccessible and mysterious as it had ever been, and unattractive except to diehard Hispanophiles.

In 1946, after ten years of fretting absence, Robert Graves returned to Majorca. "No airlines were running, no boats. The Franco-Spanish frontier was tightly closed. But an RAF friend had just helped to start an air-taxi service." He found, as Gerald Brenan was to find in Churriana, that "everything I had left behind had been looked after... Deya certainly rolled out the red carpet for me... I had to double-kiss a whole row of male and female cheeks, and tears were shed as at my departure."

Uninterested in politics, Graves was simply glad to be home. But some first-time visitors were less detached. When in spring 1947 H.M.S. Dido, taking part in the British Home Fleet's first post-war goodwill cruise in the Mediterranean, dropped anchor at Gibraltar, Able Seaman George Melly prepared to be shocked by signs of Fascist tyranny. On him, believing that the great tragedy of the Civil War was that Fascism and Stalinism had evilly combined to crush the promise of an anarchist millennium, Franco's Spain had "an almost pornographic effect... in the sense of arousing simultaneously both excitement and revulsion."

So Melly joined a coachload of naval personnel on a £6-per-head excursion arranged by the odious Spanish authorities. At the border he "shook with fervent indignation" as an officer, examining goods tipped from the panniers of an old man's donkey, "stirred them over with his jackboot and strode off." Surely, he told himself, in peasant hearts "there still smouldered the revolutionary spark which would one day burst into glorious flame."

At Jerez, after "touring a sherry factory on the estate of a marquis," the entire contingent got hopelessly drunk ("most of the ratings were 'flakers' in the lavatory"). Melly suspected that gifts of sherry and brandy were a Fascist trick to ensure that the regime's iniquities would be hidden in an "alcoholic mist," and noticed that child beggars in the streets were "dressed in rags, pitifully thin, their shaven heads covered with scabs and bald patches." But for them this was a profitable—and memorably entertaining—day. When later someone showed Melly a snapshot of these young victims, he saw that they were all "grinning like demons."

With its ancient maids tottering about in "uniforms of an Edwardian formality," paper flowers, crucifixes and devotional statuettes in corridors and bedrooms, and a large paterfamilias photograph of the Caudillo over the reception desk, the Hotel Madrid in Seville seemed to epitomize the fusty values of a dictatorship as primly pious as that of Marshal Pétain in Vichy, France. A drunken bar-crawl was followed by such breakfast-time scenes as a sailor "slapping the back of his neck several times (a Lower Deck piece of mime representing sexual congress.)" Mailing some postcards, Melly gave the stamps, featuring Franco's po-face, "a good double thumping." Touring the cathedral, he noted that female cleaners scrubbing the floor "crossed themselves and prayed every time a bell rung—proof of Pavlovian conditioning and holy brainwashing."

But holding forth in a café on the theme of "religiopolitical horse-trading" (Franco a devout Catholic, the Church gratefully Fascist), he was jolted by an incident that exposed the flimsiness of his theoretical anarchism. Shoe-shine men contrived to "pull off our heels, replace them with new ones, and were demanding the equivalent of eight shillings." Instead of welcoming this initiative as "a sign of the ability to revolt even under the most oppressive regime," Melly protested vigorously. After a heated public debate a compromise was arranged, and "with bad and blimpish grace we paid up four shillings each."

Evelyn Waugh, invited—as a Catholic convert, Franco supporter and literary celebrity—to attend a Pax Romana congress which entailed visits to Valladolid, Burgos, Vitoria and Salamanca, was far from enthusiastic about the trip. "A performance of *Lady Windermere's Fan* in Spanish, played as grand melodrama" was absurd. Most of the officials he met were obnoxious ("the mayors all seemed young shits"), the banquets tedious, Spanish academics pathetic ("the policy seems to be to appoint all literates to professorships and pay them too little to support life"). Transport breakdowns were frequent and there was little to buy in the shops. "I shall not bring back much," he wrote to his wife, "even sherry is as expensive in Madrid as in London."

But as R.A.N. Dixon, who settled in Spain in the early 1950s, remembers, a siege economy was in force and an estimated 80 per cent

Belchite in northern Aragon, wrecked during ferocious battles in
August 1937 was left in ruins as a stark reminder of the
havoc wrought by the civil war.

of imports was smuggled. Road traffic was minimal and petrol, mixed
with paraffin, was—when available—"served from steel drums with a
hand-pump." No spare parts, but "every village mechanic was a genius
at improvisation;" and using only picks and shovels, punitive gangs of
"Reds" (men who had fought on the wrong side in the Civil War) did
their best to mend the roads. Spanish-made cars were scarce, the most
affordable one being the *Biscuter*, "a two-stroke two-seater with no
reverse gear, which went downhill at tremendous speed, in the hope
that its momentum would take it up the other side."

149

In Barcelona, A. F. Tschiffely, a professional rough traveller who toured Spain in 1950, marvelled at the ingenuity of "mechanical wizards who can recondition almost any rusty Methuselah of a car" and noted that, with petrol scarce and costly, "many taxis are driven by gas, generated in veritable field kitchens fixed on the back of vehicles. Charcoal and almond shells being burnt, fumes and sometimes flames are emitted." The fancy limousines of high-ranking officials, many of them notorious *estraperlistas* (black marketeers) were the subject of cynical jokes. "CD" was said to stand for *Contrabandista Distinguido*, "PMM" (*Parque Militar Motorizado*) for *Para Mi Mujer* (For My Wife).

Having left London at a time when voyagers could take only £50 abroad and the exchange rate was 70 pesetas to the pound, Tschiffely travelled mainly by motorbike, with occasional train trips, for instance going third class to Madrid from Avila, where in the market he had seen "stacks of sections of old motortyres, used for making sandals." The train was packed, the carriages "so dilapidated that they looked more like rabbit hutches on wheels... Passengers stood in the corridor squeezed together like dried figs. The high leather-backed seats were so slippery that with every jerk people slid from side to side." Yet the mood was cheerful. He was offered wine and *chorizo*, and vigorously defended from the snooping of an officious ticket collector.

Honor Tracy, a dedicated if waspish Hispanophile, wondered at the superhuman resignation of Spaniards in transit, stoically enduring discomforts and interminable delays, and decided that it was rooted in "the dread of appearing ridiculous... the Spaniard will betray no emotion in the most hideous circumstances lest somebody should suppose him to be made of flesh and blood; and he will be more than usually stony if foreigners are present, for otherwise it might be taken as an admission that something in Spain was less than perfect."

Anthony Carson's main reactions on re-entering Spain around this time were apprehension at seeing that "half the population is armed," and delight in the branch line trains—"ancient, with tall, broken funnels," venerable relics well suited he thought, to "the crumbling, golden-brown landscape... They have a nostalgia and sense of adventure possessed by no other form of locomotion."

The poet Ted Walker, now a veteran of many Spanish sorties, has never forgotten the journey from Port Bou to Barcelona in 1955. Aged 20 and a student of modern languages at Oxford, he had been deputed to act as guide to a party which included his parents and a group of family friends. Quite a heavy responsibility, but qualms were forgotten in the excitement of this first entry into a land which for years had engaged his imagination. "What a train! Nothing to do with Europe, clearly: rather a century-old Mexican monster, complete with cow-catcher, brass belly-bands and a tall chimney belching smoke not of coal but of wood... a Wells Fargo special." He watched the driver and fireman "as I might have observed rare animals in the wild. Real Spaniards!" Waiting for departure time they were eating bread and *chorizo* with "wonderfully long, flick-bladed knives, and drank wine from squeezed leather *botas* at arm's length... the glittering parabola of liquid bridging lips and fingertips exactly as described in an ancient picaresque novel I'd been reading."

Motoring too could be pretty exciting. In 1947, driving alone, the distinguished, acidly witty author Rose Macaulay, then well into her sixties, revelled in "this fascinating peninsula which seems still, to each fresh and eager tourist, to have a wild virgin quality." But the roads were punishing. Near Gerona her front bumper "was jolted off, beginning a long series of such decadences... Throughout the nearly 4,000 miles I covered I learnt that cars are not so firmly held together as one had hoped."

The constant, manic staring to which she was subjected could be tiresome. It seemed that "señoras driving" were still regarded as "prodigies and portents, much like a man suckling a baby," and that a solitary female was "at once entertaining, exciting and remarkable, as if a chimpanzee strayed unleashed about the street." Only once, however, at Peñiscola, was she a target for more than stares and cat-calls. Some boys on the ramparts "threw down two or three tomatoes at me, which I thought moderate from a notoriously xenophobe people."

The Spanish tendency to neglect architectural splendours pleased this connoisseur of noble ruins. "In Britain our history never runs wild about the place. We prize and pet and guard it... Spain grows Roman walls and basilicas and tenth-century churches like wild figs, leaving them about in the most careless and arrogant profusion," This, she felt, was "a lordly attitude, not to be emulated by such comparative parvenus as ourselves, nor by such professional antique-owners as the Italians."

The problem, of course, was how to reach unrejuvenated antiques along equally ruinous roads. But she admits that along the way she "encountered much friendliness." So did V. S. Pritchett, who enjoyed his country bus journeys. "A barrel organ strikes up to entertain the departing, and the departure is far more like a family gathering than something on a schedule. The passengers, their lives and wishes, are more important than the bus, itself more like a dusty animal than a machine." Here in Spain the machine had somehow "been dominated by human beings and has not dehumanized them... The "backward" countries have retained the human qualities we are so anxious to lose in the interests of efficiency."

Travelling by bus from Algeciras to Seville in 1950, Laurie Lee observed "two Civil Guards, fully armed, riding with us for our protection." As in the 1870s the ranks of the bandits, "as indigenous to these parts as the wild boar and the stag," had been swollen by "an influx of escaped prisoners and political outlaws." Nothing happened. It was not "bandit weather" and these "Red guerrillas" were careful not to trouble foreigners. Despite grim warnings, Tschiffely crossed the Sierra Nevada by motorbike without mishap. But in Andalusia it was impossible not to become aware of brigands and of the legends surrounding them.

In Grazalema in 1952 Chapman Mortimer was told that some were still living in mountain caves "beautifully furnished. They have everything except documents. Good food, plenty of money, arms, and friends everywhere... People say that their children have grown up without documents and so will have to live in the hills for ever." Three

At Peñiscola in 1947, when a lone female driving a car was "a prodigy much like a man suckling a baby." Rose Macaulay was a target not only for hard stares but for "two or three tomatoes thrown down from the ramparts."

years earlier Brenan had been informed that "the whole of the river valley above Cordoba is terrorized by brigands... They raid farms and villages and carry off cattle and pigs." Though the serranía of Ronda was cordoned by police, the guerrillas (said to be grouped in regional "commands" with "intelligence units" in towns and villages) virtually controlled a large area. Occasionally they would make daring strikes to rob a bank or kidnap a wealthy citizen for ransom; as in the recent case of a Málaga businessman bagged by a bandit disguised as a Civil Guard officer. "The country people protect them and even their official enemies often have a sneaking affection for them. No Spaniard can help respecting a man who is brave and successfully defies authority."

Moorish troops, in Seville after a spell of Redhunting, relaxed in the brothels which, due to the pressures of poverty, were more numerous than ever ("the only luxury which has not gone up in price"). The Civil Guards had been given unlimited powers in troublesome areas and many suspects were "shot while trying to escape" rather than being brought to trial. Brenan remembered *guardias* in the 1930s as "grave, stern and monkish, planted in a hostile village like Knights Templar among infidels and devoted to the tradition of their service and its code of honour." Now they were ill-disciplined, corrupt and lazy, "taking their toll from black marketeers" and noticeably loath to clash with the guerrilla bands.

Pritchett reckoned that except among the great landowners of the south, and rich villa-owners "in places like the pretty town of Benidorm," *guardias* were almost universally hated, particularly in Catalonia and the Basque provinces, where they were seen as "an alien armed body who offend the pride of an independent and defeated people." Yet, aware of potentially murderous tensions, he concluded that "whatever may be said against the Civil Guards—agents of a rotten system—the Spanish state is unthinkable without some such body." Brenan, too, believed that "Spain for some time to come needs to live under an authoritarian regime."

Opinions about Franco varied. H. V. Morton diplomatically suggested that "it would be right to say that the average man admires Franco—as much as any Spaniard can admire any other Spaniard—as an honest man." Tschiffely reported that Basques hated him because he was a Galician and that Galicians hated him for the same reason. A *practicante* who had fought in the Spanish Blue Division in Russia told Brenan that the Claudillo was "a saint" unfortunately surrounded and misled by self-seekers ("if he could just step once into a bar or café and listen to what people are saying, the country would change overnight").

But even bars and cafés were forced to display notices threatening penalties for blasphemous talk. Rose Macaulay was startled by notices announcing that if a woman entered a church stockingless or in short sleeves she would be turned out, refused absolution, and denied the Blessed Sacrament. Anything savouring of liberal heresy—Picasso's paintings, the existentialist writings of Camus and Sartre—was prohibited by a philistine censorship as terrified of new ideas as the Inquisition in the Golden Age. Heavily cut foreign films, said Carson, were so unintelligible as to cause animated post-mortems

Laurie Lee, a young English poet in southern Spain.

"What happened before the girl was seen sobbing on the bed with the windows broken? Why was the man shot on the balcony?" In Seville, wrote Honor Tracy, the aged Cardinal Segura, one of Franco's favourite prelates, had forbidden dancing and "made no secret of his wish to see the Holy Office restored." In Burgos, children in sailor suits promenading with starchy nurses reminded H. V. Morton of "a long distant Kensington Gardens." Here, thought Brenan, was "an old-fashioned society—early Victorian or Second Empire, but beginning to crumble... a people not yet conquered by the pattern of industrial life with its crushing discipline."

In fact coercion was omnipresent. The nation was on a perpetual church parade since, as R.A.N. Dixon says, "the priest, in all practical matters, was more powerful than God. Upon his nod depended a job, a house, a permit or a passport." Religious fiestas had to be observed with ostentatious devotion and "the possession of a Sunday suit transcended anything to be found in the Ten Commandments." A lone woman entering a bar or walking in the street after dark was assumed to be a prostitute. On the beaches, patrolled by *guardias*, women had to wear cover-all costumes, trunks were not sufficient for men (the chest had to be hidden), and any changing had to be done in a *cabina*. Norman Lewis reported that in 1958 police in Ibiza, ordered to arrest men wearing shorts, hinted that they might "tie handkerchiefs round their kneecaps"; and as late as 1959 the National Tourist Office in London warned that "although strapless sundresses may be worn on beaches, it is advisable to cover the shoulders with a jacket or stole in towns. Cyclists may pass through towns in shorts, but if they wish to walk about without their cycles they are advised to change into more suitable clothing."

If petty regulations were plentiful, almost everything else was in short supply. Water was rationed to two hours a day, says Dixon, there were no refrigerators, no bottled gas, and in most kitchens outside the larger towns cooking was done with charcoal ("you encouraged the fire with a raffia fan"). Electricity was capricious and "in the few hotels that had a lift, the lights dimmed every time it went up or down." Sanitation was at best elementary.

Yet this pre-industrial Indian summer had its charms. Dixon doubts "if there ever existed food tastier than that which came out of the old-time Spanish kitchen." Kenneth Tynan hailed the corrida, which all through the civil war had been encouraged in Nationalist Spain, as "a rite in which on a good day heroism and beauty, the great absentees of Western Europe, may be seen happily and inextricably embraced." In Barcelona Ted Walker's father revelled in such un-Britannic luxuries as "having a shoeshine while sitting at a bar and nursing a glass of *horchata de chufas* ("Get us an ooftie-chooftie," he'd say). And Ted himself, though as an ardent young socialist he disliked "visible symptoms of an oppressive Church and State: cohorts of over-

Visiting the gypsy cave-dwellings in Granada's Albaaícin, Laurie Lee
saw the flamenco artistes as "an aristocracy" which, having
"annexed the folklore of Spain" exploited it "with a brilliant
and swashbuckling technique."

weeningly smug and superior cigarette-smoking priests at café tables; a
loaded machine-gun at each street corner," was nevertheless charmed
by a certain Edwardianesque time-slip. It was such fun to steal out of
the *pensión* late at night, "if only to indulge once again in the ritual of
summoning the *sereno* to let you back in." A peremptory hand-clap
and the key-jangling, stick-tapping functionary would approach,
"touch his peaked cap, open up for you, graciously but unobsequiously
accept the few *centimos* you tipped him; and finally bow you over the
threshold."

How, though, could any open-eyed and openhearted visitor
not hope for radical change? To Brenan, no friend of the stodgy
Welfare State, Spain seemed "a country whose road to—I do not say
prosperity—but to any humanly tolerable situation is blocked." In

Senior citizens time-killing on the steps of the monastery at Guadalupe, Estremadura in 1977—when, as Brenan remarked in a new preface to his book, the *Face of Spain* "had changed almost out of recognition."

Córdoba the "sour smell of washed tile floors, so characteristic of Andalusian *fondas*," made him feel at home, but he was shaken by a poverty far worse than he had seen before in a region long notorious for terrible deprivation. Faces coated with dirt, children of ten with wizened faces, "women of thirty already old hags... Even the lepers of Marrakesh look less wretched." Men, who by accident or conviction, had fought against Franco got no disability pension. Mutilated creatures, armless, legless, slithered about the streets.

None of this was mentioned in the press at a time when it seemed immoral that visitors should eat well, and incredibly cheaply, with starvation all around. Honor Tracy, seeing "the despair that looks out of people's eyes," reflected that "the foreigner seems to be sailing comfortably in a private craft through oceans of misery." Hordes of child beggars battened on tourists. Education, mainly provided by the Church, was sketchy. Sheila O'Callaghan, though strongly pro-Franco, admitted in *Cinderella of Europe* that half the national budget was spent on the armed forces and the police, only one-fifteenth on schools. Of around four and a half million children of school age only about half were actually enrolled. The rest begged or scavenged to help keep their families alive. Outside the big towns Pritchett saw fugitives from moribund villages living in "slums of temporary shacks built of flattened tins... The government sends the Civil Guards to burn down these horrible places, but they soon spring up again." Everywhere he was asked "Do you eat well in England?" "*No se come* — there is nothing to eat, how many times have I heard those words!"

At Almuñecar Laurie Lee watched underfed villagers straining to haul in a net filled, usually, "with a pink mass of glutinous jellyfish and a few kilos of quivering sardines... Not once did the catch fetch more than thirty shillings. Half went to the owner of the boat, the rest was divided among some twenty men." Sometimes the catch was so small that the auctioneer disdained to bid. Then the fish were shared out and "the children and the workless were left to scratch in the sand for the small fry which had passed unnoticed, and these they ate raw on the spot."

Yet all these writers were struck by a crackling intensity which, it seemed to Brenan, "charges the air with real desires and cravings." Málaga, for all its shabbiness, pulsed with an exuberance exhilarating to someone "fresh from the dull hurry of London streets and their sea of pudding faces—which often seem to have known no greater grief than that of having arrived late in the chocolate or cake queue." In the caves of Granada Laurie Lee saw the gypsies as "an aristocracy... they have annexed the folklore of the country, which they exploit with a brilliant and swashbuckling technique." Brash as this might be, it was full of energy and unfailing inventiveness. And he was excited by the street life in Algeciras, buzzing with touts offering "Gibraltar loot"—cigarettes, soap, sweets, tinned milk, coffee, jars of jam, watches—smuggled out daily from the Rock.

Spanish ebullience made Honor Tracy feel "limp, rain-washed and colourless. No one is neutral, balanced, objective, fair or "responsible," qualities possibly to be esteemed but arising from the absence of passion." Anthony Carson, who had first seen Spain as a travel courier in the 1930s, felt again "an electricity flashing from Spanish women, which fills, like a fleet of clouds, the empty submerged galleries of the mind." Brenan admired "those great jets of wiry locks... combed and dressed to rival the shine on their shoes and the gloss on their pupils... the index of the huge animal vitality of this race." For these jostling egotists, living by "a tribal or client system," it was, in the scramble to survive, a "moral duty to favour their friends at the expense of the State and to penalize their adversaries."

When Shirley Deane, an Australian, lived with her family in Nerja, it was still a touristless fishing village where, as in others along what came to be labelled the Costa del Sol, there was plenty of nothing but time. The Deanes acquired a splendid, if over-ebullient cook for less than ten shillings a week and board. The milkman drove goats along the streets, "heavy udders swinging low to the cobbles, to squirt milk expertly into each waiting dish." The street-sweepers also functioned as town-criers and official killers of mad dogs. The priest referred to the poverty of the fisherfolk as the will of God, giving help only to those who feigned piety. A widower who dared to marry a widow from another village was, with his bride, subjected to the traditional ordeal of the *cencerrada*: "They yelled and whistled and cat-called, rattled tincans strung on cords, beat sheets of tin, blew trumpet-shaped shells with a low monotonous booming, and kept it up all night." The local banking agent's son confided that he was afraid to date a local girl—"If I was seen talking twice to the same one, her parents would insist on my marrying her."

The mayor reprimanded the Deanes for crossing the square in bathing gear. The women of Nerja did not swim, and custom dictated that only on one day of the year (the feast of St. John the Baptist) could they even *walk* on the beach. Its main use was a communal latrine, there being no conveniences in the homes of the poor.

Most surprising perhaps was the way in which the comparatively wealthy and the abysmally poor accepted their destiny. The latter "lived sometimes 10 or 15 to a room, children had nits, weak eyes, TB through overcrowding and undernourishment... But they accept their poverty and the rich accept it without fear, without guilt." Oddly, in a community where the classes were so starkly defined, one was less aware of social barriers. "The rich man drinks with the poor man in the bar and they meet as equals, because one fears no change, the other hopes for none." Even the neediest families somehow contrived to spoil their children with presents they could ill afford, seeing in them their only insurance for old age—and determined not to be outdone in the competitive child-prinking of the annual fiestas.

Unchanging, seemingly unchangeable Spain. In his 1949 preface to *The Face of Spain* Brenan, as well as pleading for an end to the "anti-Fascist" economic boycott, urged more tourists to go to "one of the most beautiful countries in the world... which gives off a note unlike any other." In 1955 Honor Tracy, staying with the Brenans in Churriana, found their house, where every Saturday "a communal alms-giving took place in patriarchal fashion," still besieged by beggars.

Yet only ten years later, in a new preface, Brenan announced that "the face of Spain has changed almost out of recognition."

XI

HELLO TO ALL THAT

The impact of mass tourism

In *South from Granada* Gerald Brenan tells how in 1929 his housekeeper in Yegen was astonished, even irritated, by her first visit to the coast near Almeria. How, she asked, could the sea, which looked like a sizeable pond from the Alpujarras, be so big? Could you irrigate the land or wash clothes with it? No? Then to her mind it was a gigantic uselessness. To Maria and her like, living in the sierras or even along the sea-shore, the unholy, alliterative, tourist-beckoning trinity of sun, sand and sea (plus, in due course, sex) would have been utterly unthinkable.

But in *The Day of the Fox*, Norman Lewis' novel set in the late 1940s, a communist returning from exile to assess the potential for anti-Franco rebellion concludes that "where a generation of dedicated revolutionaries had failed, a few seasons of touristic invasions would succeed." Spain would be "democratized, hurled forcibly into this century, by the need to put on a good face for the benefit of spenders of sought-after currencies."

Lewis wrote from personal experience of a Catalan coastal village which he calls "Farol," where from 1948-50 he spent "three seasons as a part-time fisherman" and was gradually accepted into the community. Already regarding Spain as "a second homeland," he had made "a preliminary reconnaissance of the whole peninsula" before selecting Farol as supremely isolated and "not wholly freed from the customs of the Celto-Iberian past." *Voices of the Old Sea* evokes the villagers' perennial struggle to survive and their losing battle against an entrepreneur determined to transform Farol for the tourist trade, as the war-weary masses of northern Europe began to dream of a brief encounter with the Sunny South. By 1950 the battle was lost and Farol's life-style "altered more in a single decade than in the previous century." Though the Farolese detested "gypsy" Spain, they were forced to accept a Moorish-type café, pseudo-flamenco guitarrists, amplified *paso dobles* (and *perros calientes*) because that was what tourists expected.

By 1954 Farol boasted 32 hotels and Lewis retreated further and further south, eventually finding a sympathetic haven in Ibiza, again among fishermen, "dedicated artists" who cared little for money and still used hooks which were "exact replicas of those employed by the Romans." At Santa Eulalia "the sounds of the sun-lacquered plain were those of the slow, dry clicking of water-wheels turned by blindfold horses, the distant clatter of women striking at the tree branches with long canes to dislodge the ripe locust beans and the almonds... and everywhere, all round, the switched-on-and-off electric purr of the *cicadas*." But already there were signs of corruption. In 1958 Ibiza was still, despite improving communications and an influx of German and Scandinavian "gypsies," a wonderful island. Lewis estimated that, with luck, it might "go on being one for just a few more years."

Spectacularly rapid cultural erosion was to make Spain a mecca for researchers compiling theses about the impact of sudden change on a country which for so long had evaded or resisted it. In 1954, for instance, Julian Pitt-Rivers, a social anthropologist from Oxford, presented his findings after three years of research in Grazalema, a village in the Sierra de Cadiz.

The generation gap, so recently almost nonexistent, was rapidly widening. Many older inhabitants, for whom travel, except on foot, was an impossible luxury, had never been as far as Ronda, the nearest business and shopping centre. Elderly farmers, when arguing about water rights, still referred to "the traditional *señas del agua...*

When the sun's first rays struck a certain farmhouse, the right to the water changed hands. When the shadow reached the navel of the Infant Jesus which stands in a niche on another house the water must change course once more. Superstition was almost as prevalent as at Yegen in the 1920s. *Sabias* (wise women) were still much consulted. "Menstrual magic" and that sinister childstealing monster, the *sacamanteca*, were still factors to be feared.

But the tyranny of *el quedirán* (what-will-the-neighbours-say), which had ensured tight "moral unity," was loosening its grip. Young men were drifting towards the coast, mainly to the Campo de Gibraltar, where there was "a boom in the traditional industry, contraband." Under increasing pressure from the authorities in Cadiz and Madrid, age-old customs were becoming a kind of sentimental counter-culture or underground "resistance." Formal law was gradually replacing the unwritten influence of *calla'ito* (settling disputes "on the quiet" and out of court). *Patria chica* loyalties were still strong, but "state education, the radio, the cinema, easier communications and the experience of military service" were fast "carrying the culture of urban society to Alcala."

Revisiting Yegen in 1955, the Brenans found that the church clock actually worked, there was a regular bus service from Granada, old-age pensions, though tiny, had eased the lives of the poor, schooling had slightly improved, and there were plans to install modern sanitation (though as yet there was only one WC, belonging to Don José, the village shopkeeper).

There were similar stirrings in many pueblos, especially those within reach of the increasingly popular coastal strips. Anthony Carson described Sitges in the mid-1950s as "possibly the only resort where sex was allowed to be frankly European... Parisian ladies leading poodles; gigolos; fat, barefooted Don Juans." French tourists predominated, but with the irruption of youthful Scandinavians, Germans, Americans, English and Italians, Sitges was turning into "a kind of embryo training point for the Spanish Libido."

Drawn to "the free flowers of sex," Spanish youths listened

Sitges, wrote Anthony Carson, was perhaps the first coastal resort where, with the coming of frisky French tourists, "sex was allowed to be frankly European". By the mid-1950s the town was "an embryo training point for the Spanish Libido."

uncomprehendingly while typists and shop assistants from the mysterious North, bringing with them the decadent strains of jazz, talked of books, trends and personalities unknown because prohibited to them. Adventure-seeking girls surrendered with disconcerting suddenness ("underclothes and stockings and tired lipstick, and the book of Sartre, and the hot wind blowing through the hotel window"). Their attitude, though seen as contemptible—were they not foreign whores?—was also disturbingly contemptuous (was not every presentable, impoverished young Spaniard a potential lay?).

The 1954 *Everybody's Travel Guide to Spain*, published in London, still had a pioneering flavour, being addressed to those who, "seeking new and rewarding experiences, have decided to give Spain a trial." But in 1956 Horizon Holidays, a London-based package tour operator, flew the first charter-planeloads to the Costa Brava and the Costa del Sol (Majorca had already been "opened up"). This initiative was gradually followed by firms throughout northern Europe, and cut-price mass tourism made "Romantic Spain" into what the jubilant jargoneers of the travel industry called "the world's leading host nation." The 1951 figure of 1.2 million visitors had by 1961 increased to 7.4 million and by 1973 to nearly 35 million, a total slightly larger than the entire Spanish population.

James (later to be known as Jan) Morris arrived on the scene in the early 1960s and saw it with fresh eyes. Commissioned by an American publisher, but "hardly knowing Spain," he took six months off, bought a Volkswagen bus and a Linguaphone course, and "wandered around the country, writing the book in one short burst when I got home." The result was an impressionistic tour de force which, by contrast with "old hand" reactions, was not saturated with gloom at the fact that "never before had there been such a mass migration of peoples to a single destination—and this to the most resolutely insular state in Europe."

Change was on the way, not by official decree—for that would have been openly to disavow the *Movimiento's* condemnation of "materialism and egotism"—but as it were "by the service door." One could now buy an electrically-heated *mesa camilla*. Along the Calle de Alcalá in Madrid the café life which Starkie had so relished had been all but banished by grandiose banks, the diplomatic offices of the Americans ("whose vast payments in return for strategic favours are reviving the fortunes of Spain"), and the headquarters of the Directorate-General of Tourism—"whose staggeringly successful efforts to bring foreign visitors to Spain have acted as a yeast to ferment the outlooks of the Spaniards."

European capital, "spilling over the Pyrenees," was forcing "this stubborn survivor of an earlier age" to "lower its barricades." Washington Irving's raggedly proud *hidalgos* were hurrying to high-rising cities to become cogs in the industrial machine, taste the wicked joys of Western materialism, and maybe earn enough money to have a seaside holiday, like factory workers from the North. Why, they had begun to ask, should a vacation be the privilege of the rich, or of a

Aiguablava (Gerona). In 1956 the first charterplane-loads of package tourists landed on the Costa Brava and the Costa del Sol. Hotels mushroomed and by 1973 the total of foreign visitors (35 million) outnumbered the native population.

small minority of employees selected to relax in holiday camps run by the regime's "vertical unions," the *sindicatos*?

Morris' unelegiac overview, the work of a newcomer, was not shared by nostalgic Hispanophiles, old and new. Hemingway complained of "half bulls" and doctored horns. Ken Tynan considered El Cordobés, the crowd-pulling matador of the 1960s, "a clown who undermined standards even more than Manolete." Marguerite Steen found little to admire in the postwar ring and thought "tripper-ridden Spain only a degree less painful than the Spain of the Popular Front." No doubt the regime was making laudable efforts to modernize the country, but in doing so it was undermining those traditional values, that *casticismo*, it had vowed to preserve. One could, she felt, "pay too dearly for material advancement. Young Spain now imitates America in manners and morals... This is not progress, but decadence... A horrid standardization is spreading over the Western world, propagated by the tripper-trade (politely called "tourism")."

For a while she had found a haven in Puerto de la Cruz, Tenerife. But by 1955 that too had been fouled up. As in her once-beloved Granada, local youths preferred to "turn the nasty little knobs on their radios to produce a deafening blast of jazz and theme songs from films," instead of playing guitars and singing ancient ditties. The waterfront was garish with neon lights and raucous with amplified music; and "in the *dancings* Scandinavian women sought romance in the arms of waiters who flocked in from the hotels as soon as the last dinners were served."

There was something almost endearingly gauche about this transitional phase of cultural shock and linguistic confusion. Menus, like hastily-produced guidebooks and regional brochures, offered collectors' items of Spanglish. In San Sebastian Tynan noted "calamary in his own ink; anahogs in seamanlike manner; fruits of the season; tart of the house." Pamplona was "a city surrounded by smooth and odoriferous fields," while at the Pass of Roncesvalles "there took place a happening of the Ist grade in the medieval Europe."

In the early 1950s Robert Graves wrote tolerantly if apprehensively about the tourist rush ("their arrival in bulk tends to relax police regulations and decrease unemployment"). But prices, wages and rents were rising steeply and towns were "full of ugly advertisements, souvenir shops, cheap-jacks and shady adventurers." He took comfort in the fact that since passable roads were limited, the damage caused "even by the influx of the recent "Majorca, Isle of Love" period had not been too disastrous. By 1965, however, he was frankly alarmed by "the brand-new phenomenon of mass tourism—meaning charter flights, block-booking of hotels, and so clever a rationalization of ways and means that a fortnight's vacation would cost no more than an individual return fare." The result? Five thousand flights per month to an ever-expanding Palma airport throughout the summer, and the construction of more than a thousand new hotels. "Before the end of August 1964 the millionth-tourist-of-the-year had already been welcomed and given the treatment."

For most of these visitors "Spain" meant beaches, an afternoon

The bull-run at the San Fermín festival in Pamplona (Navarre) ceased to be a local affair after Hemingway's boozy celebration of it in The Sun Also Rises.

at the bullfight, posters with their names printed between those of El Litri and El Cordobés, plastic castanets, plastic dolls in regional costumes, "*flamenco* strumming by pretended gypsies," and a quick look at the monastery of Valldemosa. Daily some fifty coachloads queued to enter a "Chopin Museum" with a dubiously authentic piano, and to watch dances performed by a corps de ballet in 19th century costumes.

This might be shrugged off as harmless if exploitative farce. More serious was the ruination of Palma, the ravaging of the coast with graceless conurbations, and the fact that the lure of better-paid jobs in construction, catering, and in general "servicing" the tourist industry, had almost stripped the countryside of agricultural workers. "At Deya we now import gypsies from Andalusia, at huge expense, to get in the olive harvest. Last year some farmers let it rot on the ground. Fallen terraces are no longer rebuilt."

Olive wood was now mainly used to make bowls and boxes sold in souvenir shops, so that "as a Majorcan wag remarked, once all the trees are cut down we will have to erect plastic ones for the tourists to admire from their coach windows." Such "progress" was unstoppable: it could only be side-stepped. But for how long? "The still unexploited Majorcan hinterland is constantly shrinking as the roads improve. Where shall we retreat?" Graves did not retreat; but by 1985, when he died, a road ran close to his house and with over four million visitors a year the Majorcan economy was totally geared to the tourist trade.

In Andalusia it was still possible, if you headed away from the coast, to sample villages, inns and people much as they had been in the days of Ford and Borrow. Such was the experience of Penelope Chetwode, wife of the poet John Betjeman and daughter of a cavalry general, who in 1961 completed a six-week trek through the Sierra de Cazorla on Marquesa, a mare borrowed from the stables of the Duke of Wellington.

Some innovations she welcomed—no bed-bugs in the *posadas*, dim 15-watt light bulbs which just about enabled her to write up her daily journal. Others were less desirable—radios blaring bad *flamenco* music; ugly modern plates and "a green plastic cruet," wedding gifts displayed with distressing pride on a villager's mantelpiece ("Blast and damn all plastic consumer goods seeping in to spoil the virgin beauty of Tiscar"). In general, though, she was glad to report that "thank God the end of all Spanish things has not yet come as the great man (Ford) prophesied it would. The remoter corners of the peninsula are still "not to be enjoyed by the over-fastidious in the fleshly comforts."

Posada windows were still seldom glazed and ill-fitting shutters let in draughts. She sometimes had to relieve herself in the straw of stables, and filled her hot-water bottle with "a soup-ladle from the frying pan" since the kettle seemed to be unknown in Tiscar and Don

Diego. Rejoicing in roads too pot-holed to attract motorists, she was delighted that the only children's toys she saw, apart from skipping ropes, were balloons made of pigs' bladders. She breakfasted memorably on "pig's brains grilled in pinewood embers"; and marvelled at High Mass in the Carmelite church at Ubeda, where "the trebles sang with *cante jondo* methods of voice production which made the harmony sound odd."

The journey had been "like riding through the Garden of Eden before the Fall." But she wondered how change, alas inevitable, would affect such wholesome simplicity. How to balance between poverty and plenty so that "true happiness is not corrupted by a false sense of values?" Perhaps Gandhi's ideal of small-scale industry could be the appropriate answer for rural Andalusia? Potteries, olive presses, esparto-products, peach canning.

The "deprived" but happy children of Tiscar, Don Diego and Iodar were more likely, when they grew up, to become factory hands in Barcelona, Bilbao or West Germany, or to enter the strange new world of the Costa del Sol, than to heed the small-and-traditional-is-beautiful gospel. On the Costa they would, as James Morris wrote, be astounded by such sights as "women in trousers drinking whisky, French plumbers with luxurious trailers, gay old ladies using lipstick, girl secretaries hitch-hiking in trucks, lovers kissing on open beaches" (for the *guardias* had long ceased to apply the puritan law to foreigners).

One solo traveller, with background and motives utterly different from Penelope Chetwode's, had reason to be grateful for the softening effect of the tourist deluge. In 1964, fired by the anti-Franco tirades of Scottish miners who had fought in the International Brigades during the Civil War, Stuart Christie, an 18-year-old trainee dental technician and ardent anarchist, left Glasgow on a perilous mission. Collecting explosives at a rendezvous in Paris, he hitch-hiked to Madrid, where he was to pass the package (intended to blast Franco) to a contact. Immediately arrested, he escaped a death sentence because the British press pictured him as "an innocent young student handing out leaflets" who was monstrously doomed "to rot in a Fascist

Belsen"—and because, as he points out, his arrest as the first Brito
involved in "resistance" happened "just at the moment when Spain wa
about to plunge into the gold rush of international package tourism o
a gigantic scale." Sentenced to 20 years in gaol, Christie was release
in 1967 after some articles in The Times which set touristic alarm bel
ringing in Spanish ministries.

While Christie was doing his time, the Costa del Sol wa
acquiring a dubious fame. In 1953, said Tynan, Torremolinos had bee
"a hamlet with two hotels and a handful of pensiones." Now it was "
snake-pit... the capital of "Nescafé Society." For Honor Tracy its savin
grace, if any, was to "collect together one type of expatriate and hold i
in a kind of reservation," an idea later advanced to justify the develop
ment of Torremolinos and Benidorm as mass tourist "concentratio
camps." She later consoled herself with the illusion that "the stream c
Spanish life flows on under the nonsense, like a violin sonata all bu
smothered by a neighbouring programme of jazz." Andalusians, sh
thought, "milk the foreigner without any intention of following hi
ways... the glory of Torremolinos is to have inwardly survived its ruin.

Not for long in a place which by the mid-1960s, according t
Tynan, was "an agglomeration of bars and clubs around a centra
square... Does a barfly life spiced with amateur orgies appeal to you
notion of a holiday? If so, Torremolinos is your place... after which th
next step is Tangier, followed by a suicidal leap from a high peak in th
Canary Islands."

The cheapo *dolce vita* was, to a degree, redeemed by the pres
ence, in and around Churriana, of a "landed aristocracy" of residen
intellectuals, headed by the venerable Gerald Brenan, who might hav
been expected to react unfavourably to the Coca-Coladom so near t
their domain. But in a London *Weekend Telegraph* interview Brenan
who for a spell found the company of free-wheeling hippies a refresh
ing change from that of his fellow-aristocrats, emphasized the benefit
development, however raw, had brought to penurious peasants ("It's a
though the New York of the Red Indians had, in only eleven years
become the city of today").

Torremolinos, which by the 1960s, said Tynan, had within a decade changed from a "hamlet with two hotels" into the high-rise capital of Nescafé Society." By the 1980s, with EEC membership looming, a slogan announced that "Spain Is Not Different."

Around this time began a drive to clean up the coast for the benefit of staider tourists and retiring Senior Citizens. But the wild tempo of speculative building, littering the coast with half-finished hotels and apartment blocks and abandoned nightclubs, bars and boutiques, had the same result as that lamented by Robert Graves in Majorca. Farmers sold their land to developers. Villagers took to plaiting esparto-grass donkey heads and Don Quixotes for souvenir shops. Goatherds turned waiters or bricklayers, young women were employed as domestic servants by wealthy foreigners—who sometimes illogically complained that simple rustic charm was vanishing.

Ronald Fraser chronicled the metamorphosis of a hill village near the Sun Coast, as related by the inhabitants in interviews taped between 1957 and 1971. Gone were the "heroic" days when vendors raced each other up the slopes carrying heavy baskets of fish (100 kilos and more) strapped to their foreheads. A professional midwife had replaced amateur practitioners who, if a birth was difficult, "would tie the mother to a chair and, without anaesthetic, slit her with a silver coin." By the late 1960s the village was equipped with electric light, TV sets, fridges, washing machines, sewage disposal, butane gas cookers. Buses were frequent, bars and discos, some of them run by foreigners (including people from other parts of Spain), had opened. Yet there was an air of semi-literate boredom. Photo-novels were the chief reading matter. The streets reverberated to the racket of show-off youths revving their new motorbikes.

More than ever there was a double standard of sexual morality. *Novias* were still doomed to spinsterhood if they "strayed," or even if they broke off an engagement. Yet as one remarked, "I don't suppose it will ever be possible to find a *novio* who hasn't been with a foreign girl. There are kids of 13 and 14 who go with them now." There were other mutterings of resentment. A bank clerk deplored the moral decline ("soon we'll all be at the service of the foreigner"). An emigrant worker back from Germany was depressed by neglected fields and deserted or "dormitory" villages where most of the younger people travelled to and from work on the coast. "Spain," he commented, "is living in part off the money the emigrants send home. The tourists come here with their money and we have to leave to make money. Is that right?"

Revisiting the Canaries in 1972, Cyril Connolly was appalled by the jumbo-jet rabble and the jungle of "concrete monstrosities" built to accommodate them. In Puerto de la Cruz "Swedes everywhere, krautfrumps, corny little bars." At Maspalomas, Gran Canaria, 15 years earlier "a savage oasis of wind-blown palms and white sand," he shuddered at the sight of Playa del Ingles, "a Miami of empty apartment houses," and the Oasis Hotel, "a mammoth brown coprolith."

Only Fuerteventura, a dreary island once used as an open prison for political exiles, remained (temporarily) untouched: "the ugly sister waiting for her concrete ball-dress."

On the peninsula, the impact of mass tourism on the obvious inland target-towns was hardly less dispiriting. In Toledo James Michener was aghast at the milling confusion and ill temper of "the spiritual capital of Spain" during the summer infestation. In Cordoba and elsewhere the phoney *tablaos flamencos* staged for undiscerning tourists made him wince. Madrid was short of hotel space and the transport system was chaotic.

Brushing aside such details, James Morris assumed that Keynes' celebrated "multiplier" would beneficently operate as "every year new technical schools turn more peasants into mechanics, more investment creates more industries, the rising standard of living creates more demand for manufactured goods." But Honor Tracy was dismayed by some symptoms of comparative affluence: mini-skirted girls, "many of them half-seas over," in bars, staggering drunk peasants in Segovia... Such tokens of "a culture swiftly, dizzyingly transformed" caused her to reflect that "it is sad how a people's character melts away when the basis of it has gone" (but what was that basis? A grimly ascetic rural prison morality rooted in poverty, isolation and resignation?). Michener, noting the imitative craze which had followed the sudden breach of long-held barriers against anything that threatened "a feudal, ritualistic society," suggested that Spain was "the Japan of Europe."

A study of the Basque town of Fuenterrabia stressed the dangers of over-dependence on foreign tourism. The economy was almost exclusively geared to "the incredible sleepless frenzy of July and August, followed by ten months of gradual preparation for the reappearance of the tourists." Since 1965, when Fuenterrabia was declared an historical monument and repackaged as such it had become a sterile open-air museum "with the inhabitants as living exhibits." Yet there was always the fear that "if the tourists should decide to move on, the entire pattern of growth would come to an end... Springtime is a period of worry about this possibility."

Passing through Castile in the late 1960s I was struck by the curiously dead atmosphere of overrestored *zonas monumentales*. Gone was the pleasure of exploring ruins, so prized by Rose Macaulay. In Toledo cathedral a Frenchman with a large family protested at the fee charged to view each separate "treasure." In Merida every patch of broken, roped-off Roman mosaic had its ticket-selling attendant, the amphitheatre was cosily cocooned in tidy municipal flowerbeds. At Avila, in the warm dusk, floodlights and piped muzak issuing from regimented shrubberies trivialized the scene. I was painfully reminded of the British Tourist Authority's relentless heritage mongering, the heavy hand of the National Trust. Ted Walker, driving from Barcelona to Tarragona some years later, appreciated the fine new highway but mourned the fate of the Arco de Bara, a Roman triumphal arch near El Vendrell. Engulfed in villas and pylons, it now "stood on its own tidy island of tended oleanders, surrounded by flags of all nations... *Eheu*: the Via Augusta reduced to the rebarbative charm of the North Circular Road."

In 1973 the European oil crisis heralded recession. Factory serfdom abroad or in northern Spain was hard to come by. With rising prices, tour operators going bust, and falling tourist figures, the Costas began to feel a pinch. Gloating analysts singled out Torremolinos and Benidorm as "a warning to every government looking at tourism as an easy option... Products have a limited life... We have created a series of totally artificial towns whose ultimate fate must be to be dynamited into the sea."

Neither Benidorm nor Torremolinos has yet been dynamited. With a dozen sleek golf courses punctuating the high-rise ribbon, the Sun Coast has survived. An estimated £500 million of Arab oil sheikhs' cash, together with the loot of fugitive British crooks, have, in a sense, revived Marbella. But in 1984 headlines like "Costa del Crime," "Pillion Prowlers Rob a Briton a Day in Seville," and "Addicts Terrorize Nerja" began to appear in profusion. Instead of tobacco, hash and hard drugs were being smuggled; and the drug habit was no longer confined to a few wealthy playpeople or, as in the relatively innocent 1960s, when consuls warned tourists to "Keep Off the Grass," to foreign hippies and try-it-once squares on a holiday spree. Spanish youths, often unemployed, were in on the act and desperate for money to pay for it.

This too was a fruit of "permissive" democracy. And so, once more, as in the 15th century, the golden ghettoes of Andalusia were threatened by a host of envious have-nots. Extra police were drafted into resort areas. Security firms and manufacturers of burglar-proof *rejas* rejoiced in the crime wave as business boomed.

In Benidorm the worst menace was, and is that of moronic tourists, preponderantly British, whose drunken vandalism is dealt with by a special police squad. In Madrid the *serenos* returned to the streets armed with cans of mace and heavy coshes. An English language teacher at the university told me that she began conversation classes with the topic "How Safe Are Our Streets?", because that way everyone had a story to tell. The message "Spain Is Not Different" beneath a row of credit cards in phone booths epitomized a mimetic stampede which EEC membership will surely intensify.

Gerald Brenan, recovering from his brief flirtation with the hippy drug culture, wistfully observed that Spanish life had lost much of its savour, including the fiercely tender pride-of-place shown in such *coplas* as "Sanlucar de Barrameda/Would I could carry you folded in my pocket like a piece of paper," *coplas* which "once were sung all over Spain in the fields and cafés." Mass tourism had helped to spread mass culture, the singularity-sapping drool of TV and the transistor radio. And for many Spaniards there is no longer a *pueblo*, a *patria chica*, to celebrate.

Ironically, one method of saving inland pueblos from extinction is to spread the tourist load (and cash) by beckoning more "adventurous" or "discerning" travellers to visit these "unspoilt" places. Coastal pueblos exposed to the full mass-brunt have suffered death by suffocation. Returning to Farol in 1984, Norman Lewis found it unrecognizable. "The small, idyllic, feckless village with a population of 800 had been transformed into a "costa" town stamped out as if by

In 1958, said Norman Lewis, Ibiza was still, despite an influx of German and
Scandinavian "gypsies", a wonderful island, and with luck might remain
so "for just a few more years".

an industrial process." Fishermen now seldom fished (more profitable
to use their boats for pleasure trips) and no longer sang improvised sea-
poems. "Unctuous airport music" was omnipresent. A neon sign
suggested "Let's Go Play Cowboy Games." But at least the hinterland
was comparatively unscathed. Much of Gerona province was still
clothed in "primeval forests of pine and oak, spared because there is so
much easy money to be made in other places that it is hardly worth
while to cut them down."

Laurie Lee is disinclined to be grateful for small, fragile
mercies. In the 1950s he boldly predicted that, despite tourism, Cold
War dollars, and American military bases, Spaniards would "remain
unawed, their lips unstained by chemical juices, their girls unslacked,
their music unswung. For they possess a natural resistance to civilization's more superficial seductions." Doubts began to creep in, for
instance after visiting *flamenco* dives in Madrid, with "stamping gypsies
like glossy black mares performing to clipped Anglo-Saxon Olés." But
at the end of the decade he was still (like Honor Tracy in Torremolinos)

hoping that Ibiza would somehow survive "the miracle that has happened. Without labour or seed floating harvests of wealth now fall on the sterile island. The visitors come, asking only for charm, sunlight, and nostalgia confirmed. The island cushions them readily, like a sun-warmed lilo quickly regaining its shape when they've gone. It provides the hideout, charges a modest fee, but is neither amused nor corrupted."

Subsequent visits showed how mistaken such wishful thinking had been, in particular perhaps an incident which occurred in 1970 when he was in Segovia with a television team. The BBC van, parked outside an hotel, was stolen, and with it the old diaries he was using to write a sequel to *As I Walked Out One Midsummer Morning*. Recently he told me that in his opinion "the impact of mass tourism has been a disaster and I have preferred not to write about it. I don't go to Spain any more, I'm afraid."

SPAIN, EUROPE

The 1980s and beyond

"What if there's no there there?" quipped Gertrude Stein in a terse rephrasing of the Ford/Gautier lament.

"I could have wept for Nerja," wrote the Daily Telegraph's travel correspondent, "once so innocently picturesque on its dramatic cliff and now all but swamped by bulky new concrete blocks on one side and by self-consciously artful villa complexes on the other." And as high-rise human-hutches proliferated along the Costa del Sol, survivors from the "good old days" (of the 1950s) cursed the impact of "petitbourgeois tourist hordes" and "the sudden invasion of the International Great Unwashed that turned Torremolinos into a favourite oasis on the way to the hash-induced delights of Marrakesh," an invasion in its turn nostalgically commemorated in Michener's novel *The Drifters*.

Some writers—James Morris in the early 1960s, and more recently a bunch of energetic, young Madrid-based correspondents, among them John Hooper with his coverage *The Spaniards: a Portrait of the New Spain*—have tried to be more objective.

Large-scale tourism, said Morris, had made Spaniards realize that "theirs is not an island after all." They had begun to drink more beer and less wine, to watch football as often as bullfights, to chew bubble gum and, even while hoeing the land or herding sheep, to wear jazzily-shaped sun-glasses. American pop tunes had taken the young by storm—near Toledo he had watched "a party of convent girls dancing the twist to the music of a record-player and an audience of three giggling nuns." He had also seen the almost prehistoric lifestyle of some Andalusian peasants, living with their pigs in thatched, furnitureless huts "like kraals in the African veldt," and could not condemn a revolution that would probably sweep away such picturesque anachronisms. And yet... it was sad to reflect that such a revolution would inevitably "weaken the Spanish identity," that sense of style which had given Spain "star quality." To drive home the point Morris quotes the historian Angel Ganivet: "Spain is an absurd country... absurdity is her nerve and mainstay. Her turn to prudence will denote the end."

Hooper's bulletin reinforces that verdict. His portrait of an increasingly secularized country with machismo on the decline, permissiveness triumphant, and EEC membership as a badge of belonging, seems to bear out Joseph Baretti's contention that "we have no inherent qualities but what are common to the whole species."

One of Hooper's neighbours in Madrid had "started out as a shepherd in the province of Toledo and ended up as an electrician on the Talgo... moving from a hill cottage to a three-bedroomed flat in a block with fitted kitchens, modern bathrooms and a swimming pool." This socially mobile consumer society represents the achievement, after a century of upheaval, of Mrs Byrne's ideal ("what the Spaniards need is a realization of their wants"). Even humble workers slave and save to go abroad. In Cuenca an elderly woman who spent 12 hours a day, six days a week in a tiny newspaper kiosk told Ted Walker that she would soon be off to Scandinavia for two weeks with her sister, and that they had already been to England, Scotland, Russia and Hungary. ("It's worth being cooped up in here, if you can fly like a dove once a year!").

Alexander Jardine had urged the desirability of "making the great body of the people feel their importance. Provincial and municipal businesses and jurisdictions should be extended instead of being gradually curtailed." But would he be startled if he could see how, as

Mojácar (Almería). Half-deserted until the 1950s, when it became
a sort of Andalusian Chelsea, this hilltop village has now been
"developed" by British package-mongers.

Hooper reports, "within less than a decade one of the most centralized
nations has been carved into seventeen regions, each with its own flag
and capital, which between them can boast more than 150 'ministers'?"
And as the correspondent Robert Graham noted, in trying to please all
the regions with a wholesale largesse of closely-monitored selfgovern-
ment, Madrid offended the "historic nationalities"—Basque, Catalan
and Galician—thus playing into the hands of ETA.

Again, Hooper's summary of the effects of megalopolitan drift
abundantly justifies earlier misgivings about the social consequences of

full-blast industrialization: 11 provinces with "fewer than 25 inhabitants per square kilometre" (and one, Teruel, the first in Spain's history to register more deaths than births); ghost villages or those with a few elderly left-behinds "keeping their livestock in what were once their neighbours' cottages; an eery desolation just off the main roads, while in the cities densely-packed worker districts vibrate to harsh rock music (maybe rock *flamenco*) and the slick jargon of "a new generation as streetwise as any in Europe."

There is, says Hooper, less tax evasion, a glimmering of social conscience, far less illiteracy, and, he thinks, as memories of the civil war and fears of a military coup fade, "a new kind of Spaniard very different from the intolerant, intemperate figure of legend and history." But with massive unemployment, sketchy social security, the pressures of consumerism, and a refusal amongst the young to be grateful merely for not living under a dictatorship, *individualismo*, the "tribal or client system" half admired by Brenan and first described by Jardine, is still flourishing, though hardly more so than in other EEC countries, which is this respect are rapidly catching up with Spain.

Reminding his readers that "the Spaniards have in their time been very active," Baretti had predicted that "let the English remit of their present vigour and they will infallibly be lowered with a rapidity equal to that by which they have been raised." Spain's performance under the leadership of Felipe Gonzalez ("like a young Denis Healey going down the capitalist road") prompted Ray Gosling, another English journalist, to some variations on this theme in a radio series, *The Armada Reveng'd*, contrasting his impressions of Spain in 1955 when he flew to Alicante on a three-day half-board package (cost: £15), and thirty years later on a more leisurely tour. In 1955, he remembered, British politicians were apt to warn that if the workers didn't work harder Britain might sink as low as Spain. "How we laughed and sang on the flight and joked about Spain being so poor and backward and Fascist. Would the hotel be there, we asked, and if so would it fall down?"

Yet though some buildings, hastily constructed of watery concrete mixed with sea-beach sand, had collapsed in the early days of the tourist boom, there had been few if any examples of incompetence and corruption such as necessitated the demolition of huge death-trap tower-blocks in London and Liverpool. As for the hoary taunt that Spain was essentially African or oriental, that, said Gosling, was now much truer of Britain with its swarms of non-white immigrants. There was one mosque for rich Arabs in Marbella, but more than 300 mosques in the UK. Even the fake *flamenco* Costas were at least run by Spaniards, "like a frontier zone where the Red Indians are still miraculously in charge."

Britons, so prominent as explorers and publicists of Spain, have seldom been uncritical. A recent UNESCO warning that soil erosion due to reckless deforestation might in the next fifty years transform large areas into deserts had been anticipated by, among others, Mrs Byrne. Noticing many stretches of near-desert, she argued that reafforestation should be an urgent priority, even if it interfered with "that exquisite clearness and brilliancy of atmosphere peculiar to the scorched plains and treeless sierras."

Then there was the question of what might now be called "noise pollution." Captain George Carleton, quartered in Valencia during the War of the Spanish Succession, complained that "guitars are strum-strums little better than our Jew's harps. Yet Spaniards are perpetually at nights disturbing their women with the noise of them, under the notion and name of serenado. From the barber to the grandee the infection spreads." The Revs. Manning and Rose were irritated by incessant, raucous street cries. Ted Walker has a theory that Spaniards can put up with any amount of noise, day and night, so long as it is outside and not indoors. He had been told off by a neighbour in his hostal for typing during the siesta, at a time when in the street huge lorries with grinding brakes, roaring engines and crashing gears were creating unnoticed pandemonium. And briefly visiting Portugal, with its "English Home Counties gentility and propriety," so unlike Spain ("a country so exuberantly lived in that it is bound to get messed up and battered"), he was amazed by the Quaker-like silence in a crowded restaurant which in Spain would have been totally uproarious.

Historian and Lorca biographer Ian Gibson—born in Ireland but now a Spanish citizen who unlike Graves and Brenan prefers to live in Madrid—singled out "deafening noise" as "the greatest drawback of this in so many ways amiable country... Spanish is not spoken, it is shouted... I thought the Italians would be similarly vociferous. But they are not, and Rome is a tomb by night."

Mingling affection and exasperation, as any honest Hispanophile (or "true-born Spaniard") must, Gibson balanced lack of snobbery ("that dreadful English stand-offishness is unknown") and love of talking (or of monologue) with a marked disinclination to read books, "an almost complete disregard for Nature," and the notion that "the street is for waste disposal." More complimentarily than William Lithgow, that fiery Scot, he maintained that the Irish and the Spanish are blood-brothers with similar temperaments ("Spain is Ireland under the sun, and what could be closer to paradise than that?"). But though reckoning that to succeed in the Common Market rat-race Spain could do with "a 30 per cent all-round improvement in business efficiency," he did not wish "to see it become a sort of Germany in the sun."

Some Spaniards would have been glad to see a reduction in the annual cascade of around six million British package tourists ("pax" to the trade). As David Baird reported, the cheapness of holidays offered by hard-bargaining operators had attracted too many rowdy, drunken yobs; and the arrogant attitude of some British package-mongers had aroused hostility. One firm spent £20 million on an aparthotel ghetto-complex in Mojacar; another, with its own airline based in Spain, planned to attack the hitherto more up-market German clientele, to the fury of German tour operators and of Spanish hoteliers. One of the latter commented that "soon we'll no longer be Spanish subjects but members of the Intasun empire."

The "el gentleman ingles" image was further tarnished by a "crusading" circulation war between British tabloids over the fate of "Blackie the Donkey," the martyr of Villanueva de la Vera, scheduled, according to them, to be crushed to death "under a weight of pounding humanity" in the villagers' Shrove Tuesday *fiesta*. Such headlines as

"Savagery that Brands the Sick Soul of Spain" were followed by assertions that all Spain had to offer apart from sun was sour wine and greasy food—which it could keep, since many a decent Brit would from now on think twice about holidaying in a "proud" land capable of such fiendish cruelty.

Hundreds of thousands of them continued, nevertheless, to patronize the bullrings, where each year some 24,000 beasts were killed before a total of 31 million spectators, to the benefit of an estimated 150,000 employees of this "industry of the first order." And while the tabloid image of Spain competed with official attempts to project the country as "vibrant and creative, young and modern" (slogan: "Spain, Everything Under the Sun"), Lookout brimmed with items that did not figure in the wildest romantic forebodings: a reader in Worthing, Sussex, exhorting the editor to give more space to "the contribution made by the gay community... Spain, even more than Greece, is a mecca for gays"; Japanese tourists crossing Madrid's Plaza Mayor "wearing Sherlock Holmes deerstalkers bought in London and carrying flight bags labelled "Kinki Nippon Tours"; a big money project to build "pueblos" for Japanese pensioners in Andalusia (now categorized as "Europe's premier retirement zone" or "the California of the EEC")...

Despite some ominous stutters in the 1990s when, for instance, it was feared that "the Costa del Sol is finished," Spain's popularity as holiday destination is unabated. In 2002 there were 52 million tourists—14.5 million of these from the UK.

An astonishing invasion. But then as James Morris remarked, Spain, for four centuries so militantly insular, had previously been colonized or occupied by Phoenicians, Greeks, Carthaginians, Romans, Goths and Moors ("there never was such a palimpsest as Spain, so layered with alien influences"), a point which Lithgow had more pungently made back in the 1620s. Perhaps then, those centuries of arrested development so precious to romantic travellers were, after all, just an artificial, mythogenic interlude in the history of the Spanish Palimpsest.

Yet many parts of Spain are magnificently unpaxed and may

perhaps remain so. Even on the coast. I remember Galicia with particularly vivid delight: a tipsy peasant in Betanzos filling a bucket with
plums from a tree in his garden and, standing in the middle of a street
down which a motorcade of VIPs (accompanying the Caudillo on a
tour of his native province) had to pass, offering the fruit, with a sardonic bow, to frozen-faced, chauffeured generals; the *rías* near
Pontevedra where, emerging into mild sunshine from the monastery at
Appoyo, I watched a row of brawny, bent-over women in a field,
hacking up weeds with short-handled mattocks, singing, chattering
ribaldries, hawking and spitting, just as Jardine had seen them two centuries ago; a sunken, ferny, foxgloved lane leading to a warm, shallow
sea. In the distance two barefooted nuns with dazzlingly white coifs
digging for clams. Moored fishing boats set in a delicate cage of canes
as in a Chinese watercolour. Granite *horreos* at the beach's edge, inter-
spersed with tiny circular ticks topped by a decorative twist of hay and
a twig of apples.

In the early 1990s, some 25 years after publishing *The Road
from Ronda*, Alastair Boyd (aka Lord Kilmarnock) returned to
Andalusia, his "favourite scrap of the planet," to search for a house in
an idyllically pristine pueblo. Though, as described in *The Sierras of the
South*, dismayed by the inroads of mass culture and the tourist industry, as an incorrigible romantic he still managed to believe that "the
concept of the pueblo as Utopia remains deeply embedded."

Perhaps so, but in a land of superabundant variety there is,
really, no such thing as "a true Spain." There is the tyranny, sometimes,
of the touristic *típico*. But beyond that is a myriad of typicalities com-
posing a mosaic that each patient traveller must assemble for himself.

BIBLIOGRAPHY

All titles published in London unless otherwise stated. Most were borrowed from the invaluable London Library. For general historical background I have used William C. Atkinson, A History of Spain and Portugal (Pelican 1973); Raymond Carr, Spain 1808-1975 (Oxford University Press, 1982); and Gerald Brenan, The Spanish Labyrinth (Cambridge University Press, 1964).

Chapter 1

W. Somerset Maugham, *Don Fernando* (Heinemann 1971).

J. V. Stoye, *English Travellers Abroad* 1604-1667 (Jonathan Cape 1952).

William Lithgow, *Rare Adventures and Painefull Peregrinations* (Cape 1928; first published 1632).

Mary Fitton, *Malaga: Biography of a City* (Allen & Unwin 1971).

James Howell, *Instructions for Forreine Travel* (English Reprints 1869; first published 1642); *Familiar Letters* (David Nutt 1892; first published 1645).

John Dover Wilson, *Life in Shakespeare's England* (Penguin 1951).

Russell Chamberlin, *The Idea of England* (Thames & Hudson 1986).

T.C. Smout, *A History of the Scottish People* 1560-1830 (Collins 1969).

Lady Fanshawe, *Memoirs* (1839, but written in the 1670s).

Mme d'Aulnoy, *Travels into Spain* (Routledge 1930; first published 1691).

Daniel Defoe, *The True-Born Englishman* (1701).

Chapter 2

Voyages du Pére Labat en Espagne et Italie (Paris, 1730).

Rev Edward Clarke, *Letters Concerning the Spanish Nation* (1763).

Joseph Baretti, *A Journey from London to Genoa* (1770).

Giacomo Casanova, *Memoirs Vol 6,* "Spanish Passions" (Elek Books 1960).

Richard Twiss FRS, *Travels Through Portugal and Spain in 1772 and 1773* (1775).

Major William Dalrymple, *Travels Through Spain and Portugal in 1774* (1777).

Sir John Talbot Dillon, *Travels Through Spain* (1781).

Henry Swinburne, *Travels Through Spain in 1775 and 1776* (1787).

Alexander Jardine ("An English Officer"), *Letters from Barbary, Spain, Portugal etc* (1788).

Rev Joseph Townsend, *A Journey Through Spain in the Years 1786 and 1787* (1791).

William Beckford, *Italy, with Sketches of Spain and Portugal* (Vol 2, 1834).

Robert Southey, *Letters Written during a journey in Spain* (1797).

F. Augustus Fischer, *Travels in Spain in 1797 and 1798* (1802).

Jean-Francois Bourgoing, *The Modern State of Spain* (1808).

Elizabeth, Lady Holland, *The Spanish journal 1802.5* (Longman Green 1910).

Chapter 3

Elizabeth Longford, Wellington: *The Years of the Sword* (Weidenfeld & Nicolson 1969).

Letters and Despatches of the Duke of Wellington (1845).

Recollections of Rifleman Harris (Peter Davies 1929). Julia Page (ed), *Intelligence Officer in the Peninsula: Letters and Diaries of Major the Hon. Edward Charles Cocks* (Spellmount Ltd, Tunbridge Wells 1986).

Major-General Lord Blayney, *Narrative of a Forced Journey Through Spain and France as a Prisoner of War* (1814).

Life, Letters and Journals of George Ticknor, Vol I (Boston 1876).

Henry Inglis, *Spain in 1830* (1831, two vols).

Edgar Holt, *The Carlist Wars in Spain* (Putnam 1967).

Washington Irving, *Tales of the Alhambra*, "The Journey" (Granada, Editorial Padre Suarez 1965; first published 1832).

"A Volunteer in the Queen's Service," *A Concise Account of the British Auxiliary Legion in the Civil War of Spain* (Scarborough 1837).

A. Slidell Mackenzie, *Spain Revisited* (1836).

Chapter 4

Benjamin Disraeli, *Letters 1815-1834* (University of Toronto Press 1982).

Washington Irving, *Tales of the Alhambra,* op. cit.

Théophile Gautier, *A Romantic in Spain* (New York, Alfred A. Knopf 1926).

Alexandre Dumas, *From Paris to Cadiz* (Peter Owen 1958).

Prosper Mérimée, *Carmen and Other Stories* (Blackie 1966).

George Sand, *A Winter in Majorca* (Cassell 1956; translated and edited by Robert Graves).

Chapter 5

Richard Ford, *A Handbook for Travellers in Spain* (Centaur Press, Arundel, Sussex, 3 vols, 1966); *Gatherings from Spain* (Dent, Everyman, 1970).

Rowland E. Prothero (ed), *Letters of Richard Ford* (John Murray 1905).

Richard Ford archive at John Murray, Albemarle Street, London W.I., for a copy of the suppressed *Handbook* of 1844 and some interesting, unpublished letters.

George Borrow, *The Bible in Spain* (Dent, Everyman, 1907).

David S. Williams, *World of His Own: Double Life of George Borrow* (Oxford University Press 1982).

Chapter 6

Ford/Bensaken correspondence in Murray archive.

William G. Clark, *Gazpacho, or Summer Months in Spain* (1851).

G.G. Coulton, *Fourscore Years* (Cambridge University Press 1943).

Hans Christian Andersen, *A Visit to Spain and North Africa in 1862* (Peter Owen 1975).

Mrs William Pitt Byrne, *Cosas de España: Illustrative of Spain and the Spaniards as They Are* (1866, 2 vols).

Matilda Betham-Edwards, *Through Spain to the Sahara* (1868).

G.E. Street, *Some Account of Gothic Architecture in Spain* (1865).

Augustus Hare, *Wanderings in Spain* (George Allen 1904).

Rev Samuel Manning, *Spanish Pictures Drawn with Pen and Pencil* (1875).

Rev H. J. Rose, *Untrodden Spain and her Black Country* (1875, 2 vols); Among the Spanish People (1877, 2 vols).

Edmondo de Amicis, *Spain and the Spaniards* (1881). Havelock Ellis, *The Soul of Spain* (Constable, 1908).

Chapter 7

Rafael Shaw, *Spain from Within* (Fisher Unwin 1910).

Victor Serge, *Memoirs of a Revolutionary* (Oxford University Press 1967).

John Dos Passos, *Journeys Between Wars* (Constable 1938); *The Best Times* (Andre Deutsch 1968).

Chapter 8

Robert Graves, *Goodbye to All That* (Penguin 1965); *Majorca Observed* (Cassell 1965).

John Malcolm Brinnin, *The Third Rose: Gertrude Stein and her World* (Weidenfeld & Nicolson 1960).

Osbert Sitwell, *Noble Essences* (Macmillan 1950, Vol 5 of his autobiography).

Michael Holroyd, *Lytton Strachey: a Critical Biography* (Heinemann 1968, vol 2).

David Garnett (ed), Carrington: *Letters and Extracts from her Diaries* (Cape 1970).

Frances Partridge, *Memories* (Gollancz 1981).

Xan Fielding (ed), *Best of Friends: the Brenan-Partridge Letters* (Chatto & Windus 1986).

Gerald Brenan, *South from Granada* (Hamish Hamilton 1957); *Personal Record* 1920.1972 (Cape 1974).

Chapter 9

Tim McGirk/Mark Williams, "The Looting of Spain" (*Lookout* July 1987).

Elinor Glyn, *Letters from Spain* (Duckworth 1924).

Waldo Frank, *Virgin Spain: Scenes from the Spiritual Drama of a Great Nation* (Cape 1926).

Negley Farson, *The Way of a Transgressor* (Gollancz 1936).

Henry de Montherlant, *The Matador* (Paul Elek 1960; first published 1926 as *Les Bestiaires*).

Ernest Hemingway, *Death in the Afternoon* (Cape 1932).

Peter Alexander, *Roy Campbell: A Critical Biography* (Oxford University Press 1982).

Marguerite Steen, *Matador* (Gollancz 1934); *Looking Glass: an Autobiography* (Longmans 1966).

Karel Capek, *Letters from Spain* (Geoffrey Bles 1931).

Evelyn Waugh, *Labels: a Mediterranean Journal* (Duckworth 1974; first published 1930).

Mario Praz, *Unromantic Spain* (New York, Knopf 1929).

Kate O'Brien, *Farewell Spain* (Heinemann 1937).

V.S. Pritchett, *Midnight Oil* (Penguin 1974); *Marching Spain* (Ernest Benn 1928).

Walter Starkie, *Spanish Raggle-Taggle* (Murray 1934).

Jean Genet, *The Thief's Journal* (Blond 1957).

Laurie Lee, *As I Walked Out One Midsummer Morning* (Deutsch 1969).

Douglas Day, *Malcolm Lowry: a Biography* (Oxford University Press 1974).

Nancy Johnstone, *Hotel in Spain* (Faber 1937).

John Dos Passos, *The Best Times,* op. cit.

Norman Lewis, *A View of the World* (Eland 1986); *Jackdaw Cake* (Hamish Hamilton 1985).

Chapter 10

Arthur Koestler, *Spanish Testament* (Gollancz 1937). Robert Graves, Majorca Observed, op. cit.

George Melly, *Rum, Bum and Concertina* (Weidenfeld & Nicolson 1977).

Michael Davie (ed), *The Diaries of Evelyn Waugh* (Weidenfeld & Nicolson 1976).

R.A.N. Dixon, "Before the Big Boom" (*Lookout* December 1985).

A. F. Tschiffely, *Round and About Spain* (Hodder & Stoughton 1952).

Ted Walker, *In Spain* (Secker & Warburg 1987).

Honor Tracy, *Silk Hats and No Breakfast: Notes on a Spanish Journey* (Methuen 1957); Spanish Leaves (Methuen 1964).

Anthony Carson, *Poor Man's Mimosa* (Methuen 1962).

Rose Macaulay, *Fabled Shore* (Hamish Hamilton 1949).

V.S. Pritchett, *The Spanish Temper* (Chatto & Windus 1954).

Laurie Lee, *A Rose for Winter* (Hogarth Press 1955).

Chapman Mortimer, *Here in Spain* (Cresset Press 1955).

Gerald Brenan, *The Face of Spain* (Turnstile Press 1950).

Kenneth Tynan, *Bull Fever* (Quality Book Club 1956).

Sheila O'Callaghan, *Cinderella of Europe* (Skeffington 1951).

Shirley Deane, *Tomorrow is Mañana* (John Murray 1957).

Chapter 11

Gerald Brenan, *South from Granada* op. cit. ; *Thoughts in a Dry Season* (Cambridge University Press 1978).

Norman Lewis, *The Day of the Fox* (Cape 1955); *Voices of the Old Sea* (Hamish Hamilton 1984); *A View of the World* op. cit.; "A Lost Village on the Costa Brava" (*Sunday Times Magazine* 2 Sept 1984).

Julian Pitt-Rivers, *The People of the Sierra* (Weidenfeld & Nicolson 1954).

Anthony Carson, *Poor Man's Mimosa* op. cit.

Louis Turner and John Ash, T*he Golden Hordes: International Tourism and the Pleasure Periphery* (Constable 1975).

James Morris, *The Presence of Spain* (Faber 1964); letter to author, Dec 1985.

Kenneth Tynan, *The Sound of Two Hands Clapping* (Cape 1975); *Right and Left* (Cape 1967).

Ernest Hemingway, *The Dangerous Summer* (Hamish Hamilton 1985).

Marguerite Steen, *Pier Glass: More Autobiography* (Longmans 1968).

Penelope Chetwode, *Two Middle-Aged Ladies in Andalusia* (Murray 1963).

Stuart Christie, *The Christie File* (Partisan Press/ Cienfuegos Press 1980).

Laurie Lee, *A Rose for Winter* op. cit. ; *I Can't Stay Long* (Deutsch 1975).

Honor Tracy, *Spanish Leaves* op. cit.; *Winter in Castile* (Eyre Methuen 1973).

Ronald Fraser, *The Pueblo: a Mountain Village on the Costa del Sol* (Allen Lane 1973).

Cyril Connolly, *The Evening Colonnade* (David Bruce & Watson 1973).

James Michener, *Iberia* (Secker & Warburg 1968).

Dafydd J. Greenwood, "Tourism as an Agent of Change: a Spanish Basque Case" (Fuenterrabia), (*Ethnology* January 1972).

Ted Walker, *In Spain* op. cit.

Epilogue

Titles of books by Baretti, Jardine, and Mrs Byrne to which reference is made have already been listed.

Elisabeth de Stroumillo on Nerja (*Daily Telegraph* 11 July 1981).

John Hooper, *The Spaniards: a Portrait of the New Spain* (Viking 1986).

Robert Graham, *Spain: the Change of a Nation* (Michael Joseph 1984).

Ray Gosling, *The Armada Reveng'd* (BBC Radio 4, 1986).

Captain George Carleton, *Memoirs* (1728). Ted Walker, In Spain op. cit.

INDEX OF AUTHORS

For a free catalogue
of all our books on Spain
contact:
Santana Books,
Apartado 422,
29640 Fuengirola (Málaga).
Phone 952 485 838.
Fax 952 485 367.
Email: sales@santanabooks.com
www.santanabooks.com

UK Representatives
Aldington Books Ltd.,
Unit 3(b) Frith Business Centre,
Frith Road, Aldington,
Ashford, Kent TN25 7HJ.
Tel: 01233 720 123. Fax: 01233 721 272
E-mail: sales@aldingtonbooks.co.uk
www.aldingtonbooks.co.uk